Terrier Hall

BEST OF BRITAIN'S

Coast

A SPECTACULAR JOURNEY AROUND BRITAIN'S SHORES

Produced by AA Publishing
© Automobile Association Developments Limited 2004
Maps © Automobile Association Developments Limited 2004.
Crown copyright. All rights reserved. Licence number 399221.

Published by AA Publishing (a trading name of Automobile Association Developments Limited,
whose registered office is Millstream, Maidenhead, Windsor SL4 5GD; registered office 1878835)

A 01911A

ISBN   0 7495 4047 8

A CIP catalogue record for this book is available from the British Library.

Produced for AA Publishing by *The Bridgewater Book Company*

Printed and bound in China

PICTURE ACKNOWLEDGEMENTS

All photographs are held in The Automobile Association's own library with
contributions as follows:

t (top), b (bottom), c (centre), l (left), r (right), bg (background)

S Anderson 112l; A Baker 60r; P Baker 9b, 10, 44, 46b, 47l, 50br, 52t, 67; S Bates 141;
J Beazley 5, 90tl, 91 br, 92, 93, 94, 95t, 96, 103br; 113; A Besley 23, 30, 31t, 35; M
Birkitt 69, 70; J Blandford 100r; D Burchill 114; I Burgum 24tl, 126, 127, 131r, 135,
137, 139, 140; M Busselle 6l, 24bg tl, 63r, 64, 68l, 68r; 90bg tl, 90tc, 102bg tl; J Carnie
110l, 111; D Croucher 122, 123; S Day 13b, 56, 115t; P Davies 72, 79; E Ellington 107;
D Forss 58br; 59; V Greaves 115b; D Hardley 108; J Henderson 7r, 99l; A Hopkins
77b, 87, 88l, 89, 95b; J Ingram 11; R Ireland 49, 53, 54t, 54cr, 136l; N Jenkins 119t, 129,
134tr, 142, 143t, 143b; C Jones 8, 22, 25tr, 25cr, 28br, 29tl, 39, 43t, 43b, 45, 46t, 50bl,
51, 90tr, 91l, 116/117, 118b, 120/121; J Jorgenson 118t, 125l, 125r, 128; M Jourdan 25l,
52b, 55; A Lawson 13t, 16, 48; T Mackie 3, 25bg tc, 25bg tr, 24bl, 73tl, 73cr, 74l, 74r, 75,
78t, 81, 82, 83, 91bg tr, 103bg tr, 144; S & O Mathews 58tr, 63l, 65r, 78b, 80, 103tr; G
Matthews 124l, 124r; S McBride 57; J Miller 6r, 24bg tc, 62, 90bg tc, 102bg tc; C
Molyneux 134b, 138; J Morrison 24tc, 85, 86; R Moss 14/15, 18, 19, 25bg tl, 26, 27,
28bl, 31b, 33l, 34, 36/37, 38, 91bg tl, 103bg tl; J Mottershaw 84; R Newton 25br, 119b;
K Paterson 97r, 102 tr, 102bl, 109, 112r; N Ray 32, 41; T Souter 76, 77t; R Surman
29cr, 88r; M Taylor 97l, 98, 99r; T Teegan 9t, 20, 24bg tr, 90bg tr, 102bg tr; R Tenison
21, 29b, 33r, 40, 42; M Trelawny 60l; W Voysey 17, 24r, 50tr, 61, 65l, 66t, 66b, 71b; R
Weir 100l, 102tc; S Whitehorne 101, 104b, 105; H Williams 47r, 90bl, 106, 130/131; P
Wilson 91tr; J Wyand 12.

Cover: Mupe Bay near Lulworth Cove – Richard Ireland
Inside Flap, Cardigan Bay from Cemaes Head on the Pembrokeshire Coastal Path –
Ian Burgum
Spine, Eastbourne – John Miller
Back Cover bl, Eastbourne – Michael Busselle
Back Cover bc, Clacton on Sea - Wyn Voysey
Back Cover br, Beachy Head - John Miller
Back Cover bg, beach huts at Wells-Next-The-Sea, Norfolk -Tom Mackie

Contents

*100 of the country's best coastal spots, listed from southern
England, up the eastern and northern coasts around Scotland
and down the Welsh coast*

Features

*Whether you're a fan of sunbathing, entertainment or water sports,
Britain seaside resorts have something to offer everyone.*

*Discover the fascinating town of Lyme Regis, famous for its fossils,
and follow the guided walk to explore its surrounding hills and harbour.*

*Learn about some of Britain's most compelling and historical
lighthouses.*

*As you explore Britain's coastline you will spot many beautiful birds.
Here is a glimpse of some of those you may encounter on your travels.*

BEACH HUTS AT SOUTHWOLD

Location Map
Around Britain's coast

Coastal spots by region, including page numbers

The Minch

Bonar Bridge

Gairloch

Shieldaig

Plockton

Inverness

Peterhead

Moray Firth

Isle of Skye

Aberdeen

Fort William

Dundee

Inveraray

Lower Largo

Glasgow

Edinburgh

Berwick-upon-Tweed

Lindisfarne Castle

Farne Islands

Bamburgh

Brodick

Ayr

Culzean Castle

Dunstanburgh Castle

Portpatrick

Carlisle

Newcastle upon Tyne

Marsden Bay

Solway Firth

Middlesbrough

Whitby

Robin Hood's Bay

Scarborough

Morecambe

Irish Sea

North Sea

Blackpool

Leeds

Kingston upon Hull

Liverpool

Manchester

Llandudno

Conwy

Llanddwyn Island

Menai Bridge

Portmeirion

Birmingham

Cley next the Sea

Holkham

Hunstanton

Wells-next-the-sea

Cromer

Great Yarmouth

Cardigan Bay

Aberystwyth

Southwold

Aldeburgh

Strumble Head

St David's

Fishguard

Milford Haven

Skomer

Skokholm

Tenby

Swansea

Pembrokeshire Coast National Park

Gower Peninsula

Cardiff

Bristol

LONDON

Harwich

Clacton-on-Sea

Margate

Bristol Channel

Hartland Quay

Bude

Clovelly

Boscastle

Tintagel

Crackington Haven

Padstow

Port Isaac

Exeter

Newquay

Bedruthan Steps

Godrevy Head

St Ives

Zennor

Hayle

Fowey

Polperro

Beer

Sidmouth

Lyme Regis

Weymouth

Chesil Beach

Torquay

Brixham

Plymouth

Slapton Sands

Lulworth Cove

Southampton

Isle of Wight

Bosham

Portsmouth

Beachy Head/ Seven Sisters

Brighton

Eastbourne

Hastings

Rye

Folkestone

Strait of Dover

Land's End

Helford

Marazion

The Lizard

Falmouth

English Channel

Heritage Coastline

N

Introduction

England, Scotland and Wales form Britain – the largest island in Europe, with a coastline some 6,000 miles (9,655km) long – incorporating cliff and headland, rock and shingle, dune and marsh.

Britain is a maritime country with a rich maritime heritage, and the sea has exerted a profound influence on the country's history and character. Harbours and coves, and towns and villages all round the coast are the products of centuries of wresting a living from the sea. Britain's historic greatness rested on sea power and seaborne trade. The British Empire, the largest in the world's history, was controlled over vast distances by command of the sea. The sea in its every mood, from violent storm to sullen swell to flat calm, from sparkling blue to rain-washed grey, is a familiar companion to British life.

The miles of coastline run through a rich variety of scenery, each with its own magic. Along the north Devon and north Cornwall shore a line of adamantine cliffs rears up against the fury of the Atlantic, the immovable object confronting the irresistible force. Another titanic cliff barricade guards the Yorkshire coast against the North Sea. In Wales the craggy cliffs of the Lleyn Peninsula and the

PREVIOUS PAGE:
BAMBURGH CASTLE

BRITAIN'S COASTLINE
IS PUNCTUATED BY
ITS UNIQUE LANDMARK
PLEASURE PIERS.

STRIPED DECKCHAIRS
ARE A TRADITIONAL
FEATURE OF BRITAIN'S
COASTAL RESORTS.

Pembrokeshire coast keep the Irish Sea at bay, while down
the length of Scotland's beautiful and romantic western
coast the lochs ripple sweetly below the mountains as the
sun sinks in blood-red glory beyond the Western Isles.

By contrast, along the flat and muddy Essex coast the
sea has reached far inland to make a lonely wilderness of
creeks and marshes, beloved of yachtsmen and wildflowers.
Up the lowlying Suffolk shore the melancholy pebbles roar
and rattle with the changing tides. A chain of delightful
sandy beaches stretches up the long, smooth flank of
Northumberland, and on the Lancashire coast the vast

sands of Morecambe Bay glimmer under a colossal sky.

Each varied shoreline has its plant life and wildlife to discover, and coastal paths conduct the walker close to much of Britain's coast. On the way is an engaging parade of naval bases like Plymouth, seaports like Harwich, venerable old trading towns like Rye, and picturesque little fishing harbours, with their boats and nets and wheeling gulls. There are castles and towers, lighthouses and piers and smart Regency seaside resorts like Brighton.

MUCH OF BRITAIN'S LONG COASTLINE IS TRANQUIL AND UNDEVELOPED.

Clovelly
Devon
12 miles (19km) west of Bideford

Everyone's heard about Clovelly. It's an extraordinary place – almost a folly itself – best seen very early in the morning, or at the end of the day or in mid-winter when most of the visitors have gone home and it has an almost timeless feel. It clings precariously to the wooded cliffs on the long, virtually uninhabited stretch of inhospitable coastline between Bideford and Hartland Point. Once famous as the village where donkeys were used to carry goods and people from the quay up the perilously steep cobbled village street (the bed of an old watercourse), today it is best known as a tourist trap. Most people drive to the village and are drawn into the visitor centre car park at the top – but it's much more satisfying to walk in along the coastal path from the National Trust lands at Brownsham to the west. The two 17th-century farmhouses of Lower and Higher Brownsham lie just inland from one of the most unspoilt sections of the North Devon coastline. Although the walk is rarely out of the trees, you can still hear the pull and drag of the waves on the shingle beach far below.

Clovelly Court dates from c1740, when the Hamlyns bought the manor from the Carys, but was remodelled in Gothic style in 1790–5. The much-restored 15th-century All Saints Church has a Norman porch, dating from c1300, and many monuments to the Cary and Hamlyn families. Sir James Hamlyn, who died in 1829, was responsible for the building of the Hobby Drive, which runs for 3 miles (5km) along the cliffs east of Clovelly, and from where there are fantastic views of the harbour, 600ft (183m) below.

CLOVELLY'S COLOUR-WASHED COTTAGES CLING TO THE STEEP NORTH DEVON CLIFFS ABOVE THE HARBOUR.

DON'T MISS
KINGSLEY MUSEUM
14TH-CENTURY HARBOUR
FISHERMAN'S COTTAGE AND CRAFT WORKSHOPS
AUDIO-VISUAL THEATRE

WESTWARD HO!

Clovelly's fine quay was built by George Cary, the 16th-century squire whose son William plays a prominent and dashing role in Charles Kingsley's *Westward Ho!* (1855). It was this popular historical novel that first marked Clovelly as a tourist attraction and the world suddenly became aware of this remote village's existence. Up till then Clovelly had been primarily reliant on herring fishing for its main source of income. Kingsley knew the village well – his father was Rector of Clovelly in the 1830s and Charles spent part of his boyhood at the rectory. Charles Dickens also mentioned Clovelly in *A Message from the Sea* (1860), so extending its newfound popularity.

BOATS DRAWN UP ON THE SHINGLE ARE A REMINDER OF CLOVELLY'S EARLY SOURCE OF INCOME.

THE TOWN'S COBBLED STREET IS SO STEEP THAT AT ONE TIME DONKEYS WERE USED TO TRANSPORT PEOPLE AND GOODS UP AND DOWN IT.

Hartland Quay
Devon
6 miles (9.5km) west of Clovelly

CRAGGY ROCKS RUN IN
JAGGED LINES TOWARDS
THE TREACHEROUS CLIFFS
OF HARTLAND.

Devon's northwest tip is characterised by an extraordinary change in the nature of the coast. The cliffs along the coast from Clovelly, to the east, although high, are calm and flat-topped, yet turn the corner at Hartland Lighthouse and you enter a different world. You can understand why this area is peppered with shipwrecks. The coastal path to the south of the point crosses a mass of vertical tiltings and contortions, caused by lateral pressure on the earth's crust around 300 million years ago. *Hartland* means 'stag island', although the area is a peninsula, and the feeling of space and remoteness is made even stronger by the fact that on a clear day there are inviting views of Lundy Island, rising majestically out of the sea 10 miles (16km) offshore. On stormy days, Lundy mysteriously disappears into a blanket of mist and spray. The island is basically a great lump of flat-topped granite: 52 million years old, 450ft (137m) high, 3 miles (5km) long and only $\frac{1}{2}$ mile (800m) wide. Hartland Quay dates back to 1586. Cargoes of coal, lime and timber were landed here, and in 1616 lead was brought in for repairs to the roof of St Nectan's Church at Stoke. The quay was active until 1893, and once abandoned was soon destroyed by the ravages of the sea. The buildings have been converted into the Hartland Quay Hotel, museum and shop.

Bude
Cornwall
12½ miles (20km) south of
Hartland Point

There are few more exhilarating beaches than
Bude's Summerleze when the sea rolls on to the
sand in long, unbroken waves. However, there is more
to Bude than its beautiful beaches. The Bude Canal
shaped much of the immediate hinterland of Bude
Harbour and is now a popular attraction. The canal was
built in the early 19th century to carry calcium-rich
sand to the inland farms, where it was used to enrich
the soil. The canal reached nearly to Launceston, but its
full potential was never realised and its use declined by
the middle of that century. The history of the canal is
illustrated in the Bude-Stratton Museum at the Old
Forge on the Lower Wharf.

   Around the seaside resort of Bude, the cliff edges
especially provide a unique refuge for many fascinating
wildflowers. The flat cliff land supports a wildflower
fiesta that turns the cliff top into a riot of colour in
spring and early summer. On the outskirts are Crooklets
Beach and the cropped grasslands of Maer Cliff and
Maer Down. In spring the dominant flower here is the

BUDE'S LONG SWEEP
OF SAND MAKES
IT A POPULAR
HOLIDAY RESORT
FOR FAMILIES.

BUDE CANAL, WHICH LEADS TO THE TOWN'S HARBOUR, WAS CONCEIVED IN 1774 BY CORNISHMAN JOHN EDYVEAN.

spring squill, whose distinctive powder-blue flowers are dotted across the grass. Other early plants that flourish here are the lilac-coloured early scurvy grass, the pink thrift and white sea campion. At Northcott Mouth the cliffs give way to a wide stony beach.

You are quite likely to see a number of butterflies along the cliff tops, including the meadow brown, probably Britain's commonest butterfly, its name a perfect description of its dusky colour. You may also see the common blue, a small butterfly with an almost lilac tinge, and the glamorous painted lady, with its tawny-orange wings and black-and-white markings. The painted lady's main habitat is southern Spain and North Africa, from where large swarms often migrate north in April and May, finding no difficulty in crossing the English Channel.

THE PAINTED LADY BUTTERFLY MAY BE SEEN IN SUMMER.

Crackington Haven

Cornwall

9 miles (14km) south of Bude

Crackington Haven has given its name to a geological phenomenon, the Crackington Formation, fractured shale that has been shaped into incredibly twisted and contorted forms. On the sheared-off cliff faces of the area, you can see the great swirls and folds of this sedimentary rock that was metamorphosed by volcanic heat and contorted by the geological storms of millions of years ago. Even the name 'Crackington' derives from the Cornish word for sandstone, *crak*. The very sound, in English, hints at friability and dramatic decay. Scripted across the face of the vast cliffs traversed by this walk are the anticlines, (upward folds) and synclines (downward folds) that are so characteristic of these great earth movements.

During the 18th and 19th centuries, Crackington Haven was a small port, landing coal and limestone and shipping out local agricultural produce and slate. Small coastal ships would anchor off the beach, or settle on the sands at low tide, in order to exchange cargoes. Plans to expand Crackington into a major port were made in the early 19th century. The grandiose scheme aimed to build huge breakwaters to protect Crackington and the neighbouring Tremoutha Haven from the huge Atlantic swells. Quays and docks were to be built inside the protected harbour. A rail link to Launceston was proposed and a small new town was planned for the haven, which was to be renamed Port Victoria.

CRACKINGTON'S SCANT AND ROCKY RIDGES

CONTRIBUTE TO A DRAMATIC COASTLINE.

CRACKINGTON HAVEN
NESTLES COMFORTABLY
AT THE FOOT OF SHEER
SANDSTONE CLIFFS.

As with many development plans of the time, the scheme did not materialise, otherwise the Crackington Haven of today might have been a dramatically different place. Along the open cliff south from Crackington you can see the remarkable nature of the geology. Looking back from Bray's Point, the massive contortions in the high cliff face of Pencannow Point on the north side of Crackington are clearly visible. The path leads above Tremoutha Haven and up to the cliff edge beyond the domed headland of Cambeak. From here there is a breathtaking view of the folded strata and quartzite bands of Cambeak's cliffs.

A short distance further from Crackington Haven is Strangles Beach, where there are fantastic natural features such as Northern Door, a promontory of harder rock pierced by a natural arch where softer shales have been eroded by the sea. Inland from here is a line of low cliffs set back from the main cliff edge, caused by a landslip where the cliff has slumped towards the sea.

Boscastle

Cornwall

5 miles (8km) southwest of Crackington Haven

DON'T MISS

WILLAPARK IRON-AGE FORT

THE VALENCY VALLEY

ST JULIOT'S CHURCH

The sea can surge in and out of Boscastle Harbour in a menacing way, entering between looming cliffs of slate and shale. The outer walls of the harbour are always damp with the sea and the salt air. Most of the area is owned by the National Trust, as are the adjoining cliff lands of Willapark to the south and Penally to the north. The blowhole in Penally Point, the headland on the northern side of the harbour entrance, is known as the Devil's Bellows and, when tide and sea conditions are right, it throws a spectacular spout of spray across the harbour entrance.

Boscastle was a busy commercial port throughout the 19th century – sea transport was usual throughout north Cornwall until the railway arrived in the 1890s. Up to 200 ships called at Boscastle in any one year, carrying coal and limestone from South Wales, wines and spirits, general goods, and even timber from Bristol. Cargoes out of Boscastle included china clay and slate and manganese from a mine in the Valency Valley above the village. Boscastle Harbour was always difficult to enter and sailing vessels had to be towed through the entrance by eight-man rowing boats and horses on tow paths.

The valley of the River Valency runs inland from Boscastle through deep woods, a peaceful contrast to the threatening sea.

THE RIVERS VALENCY AND JORDAN
FLOW INTO BOSCASTLE'S HARBOUR.

Tintagel
Cornwall
4 miles (6km) northwest of Camelford

DON'T MISS

TINTAGEL CASTLE

OLD POST OFFICE

KING ARTHUR'S HALL

According to legend, the mighty King Arthur was conceived at Tintagel Castle. Through the contriving of Merlin, the master magician, the beautiful Duchess Igraine of Cornwall was deceived into thinking that the man in her bed that night was her husband, the Duke, when it was actually Uther Pendragon, High King of Britain. This link with the Arthurian legends inspires the many souvenir shops in the village. However, the remains of Tintagel's castle are

spectacularly romantic – they stand on a towering crag, high above the sea and are reached by a narrow causeway and precipitous steps from the headland, which was also fortified.

Recent archaeological work here suggests that this immensely impressive place was an important royal site in the post-Roman period – the period of Arthur – and was perhaps the crowning place of the British high kings. The castle ruins are much later, dating from the 12th century onwards.

The isolated church of St Merteriana and the charming medieval Old Post Office are well worth seeing, too. Also in the village is the weird and wonderful King Arthur's Hall, with stained-glass windows portraying the Knights of the Round Table.

TRAGIC LOVERS

Tintagel is linked with the tale of Tristram and Iseult, an originally separate story that was drawn into the Arthurian legends. Tristram of Lyonesse was the nephew and chief champion of King Mark of Cornwall, who held court at Tintagel, and it was here that he brought the lovely Iseult from Ireland to be Mark's queen. Tragically, Tristram and Iseult fell irresistibly and hopelessly in love. In the end, when the two lovers died, the sorrowing Mark buried them both at Tintagel.

TINTAGEL OFFERS SOME BREATHTAKING VIEWS FROM ITS COASTAL FOOTPATHS AND THE ARTHURIAN CONNECTION ENHANCES THE MYSTERY OF THE RUGGED COASTLINE.

LEFT: THE OLD POST OFFICE (NATIONAL TRUST) AT TINTAGEL IS HIGHLY ECCENTRIC.

Port Isaac
Cornwall
9 miles (15km) southwest of Tintagel

Where the stark cliffs of the north Cornwall coast stand guard against the relentless sea between Rumps Point and Tintagel Head, the little harbour of Port Isaac is sheltered by the bulk of Lobber Point. Whitewashed cottages crowd the narrow streets and lanes, one of which is so cramped that it is graphically called Squeezebelly Alley. Fishing boats, nets and the cries of gulls lend atmosphere to a port from which Delabole slate was once shipped.

Port Isaac was a thriving fishing harbour in the 19th century, when the vast shoals of pilchard made their regular appearances along the Cornish coast. They come no more, and the little town now depends on visitors for its living. The handsome old parish church is to the south at St Endellion, and a couple of miles to the east the double ramparts of Tregeare Rounds can be seen (up to 50ft/17m wide). This Celtic hill fort was excavated in 1904, and pottery from shortly before the Roman period was discovered. The fort has been identified as the Castle Terrible of Thomas Malory's 15th-century epic *Morte d'Arthur* – the spot where Uther Pendragon besieged the Duke of Cornwall.

Padstow

Cornwall

5 miles (8km) northwest of Wadebridge

DON'T MISS

PRIDEAUX PLACE

THE OBBY OSS
(HOBBY HORSE)
MAY DAY FESTIVAL

RICK STEIN'S SEAFOOD
RESTAURANT

THE PRETTY HARBOUR
AT PADSTOW HAS BEEN
A SHIPPING REFUGE
FOR CENTURIES.

Padstow is a likeable, good-natured town in a fine position on the Camel Estuary. It was a busy trading port from the earliest times, and Welsh and Irish saints of the Dark Ages landed here. The town's maritime history is a noble though often tragic one. The shifting sand bar across the mouth of the estuary, the Doom Bar, is dangerous at times. Records show that over 300 vessels were wrecked here between 1760 and 1920. At low tide, a vast expanse of sand sweeps away from Padstow, shading to gold towards the sea and to honey-coloured mud towards the inner estuary. At high tide it is all glittering water.

The busy harbour has been modernised but, in keeping with traditional style, retains its picture-postcard appearance. The cluster of buildings around it, and the maze of streets and warren of narrow passageways behind it, maintain a pleasant coolness on sunny mornings.

The route of the old railway line, closed in 1967, is now the Camel Trail, a walking and cycle route. North of Padstow is Stepper Point, the fine headland at the entrance to the estuary. The Saints' Way, *Forth an Syns* in Cornish, is a 28-mile (45km) walking route from Padstow to Fowey. It is a delightful route that can be walked in two days.

Bedruthan Steps

Cornwall

6 miles (10km) northeast of Newquay.

Access to the beach at Bedruthan has been difficult over the years because of the crumbling nature of the cliffs, but the National Trust has built a secure stairway from the cliff top at Carnewas. The famous steps are the weathered rock stacks that stand in bold isolation amidst the sand. Bedruthan Steps are the result of sea erosion on the caves and arches in the friable slate cliffs. They have colourful local names, such as Queen Bess, Samaritan Island and Diggory's Island. According to local legend, a mythical giant, Bedruthan, was reputed to use the great stacks as stepping stones; but to nowhere in particular, it seems. There is a shop and café on the cliff top in what was once the office building of the old Carnewas iron mine. Cream teas and other Cornish delights are the order of the day.

THE MASSIVE ROCK FORMATIONS ALONG THE BEACH ATTRACT MANY VISITORS.

Newquay
Cornwall
11 miles (18km) north of Truro

DON'T MISS	
DON'T MISS	NEWQUAY'S ATLANTIC
THE BEACHES	SWELL MAKES IT
BLUE REEF AQUARIUM	BRITAIN'S PREMIER
NEWQUAY ZOO	SURFING CENTRE.

Newquay today is geared unashamedly to its splendid beaches, of course, and boasts many hotels and guesthouses. But the town was once Porth Lystry, the 'boat beach', and its harbour, or 'new quay', dates from 1439, when it was decided that it would be a safer landing place for vessels than the Gannel Estuary. Business at Newquay was brisk, with much pilchard fishing, and copper and china clay export in later years. At the harbour today there is a strong sense of the old Newquay. The seafaring trips on offer give a taste of the town's sea-going traditions.

Newquay's broad, busy streets filled with shops, pubs and clubs contrast with quiet corners in flower-filled parks and gardens. Its beaches are the most extensive and accessible in Cornwall. They run in a line to the north, from Towan Beach, in front of the town, through Great Western and Tolcarne Beaches to Lusty Glaze and Porth. Further north again is Watergate Bay, all shining sand and glittering sea, with a pause at Berryl's Point before the popular family beach of Mawgan Porth is reached. The Atlantic swells make Newquay's impressive Fistral Beach a leading surfing venue.

LEFT TO RIGHT: BATHERS AT WHITESAND; KIDS AT SCARBOROUGH; PUNCH & JUDY, CLACTON-ON-SEA; BELOW: WELLS-NEXT-THE-SEA

Seaside Holidays

The seaside holiday is a modern invention. Until the 18th century, the sea was generally distrusted as a dangerous and disagreeable element. A change of attitude stemmed more from concern with health than with fun and doctors promoting the beneficial effects of sea water and sea air.

The immediate ancestor of the seaside resort was the spa. Towns like Bath offered a combination of mineral waters and smart socialising. Scarborough was a spa by the sea, and by 1735 visitors were nervously entering the briny. The new fad spread to Brighton, which by personal appointment to the future King George IV blossomed as the smartest of resorts. His father, George III, went to Weymouth for his health in 1789 and the grateful town prospered under the mellifluous name of Melcombe Regis. Cromer was attracting rich Norwich families by this time, and Margate was a magnet for London trippers.

From the 1840s on, as the railways spread their tentacles to almost every corner of the country, visitors could reach even remote spots. Places with sandy beaches had a natural advantage, from Newquay to Ayr. So did places with a high sunshine count, such as Torquay and the Isle of Wight resorts. Landowners and developers moved to turn empty beaches and insignificant harbours into sources of profit.

The railways made it possible for ordinary working people to get away to the seaside for a day and, as holidays steadily lengthened, for a week or more. Resorts like Clacton and Skegness swelled into cheerful, noisy, unabashedly vulgar magnets for the masses.

Blackpool reached its peak number of visitors in the 1960s. It still does excellent business, but today's resorts face a challenge from changing habits: the vogue for holidays abroad and a move away from spending the whole holiday in the same place. The traditional seaside resort may become a thing of the past, but it was fun while it lasted.

A FUNFAIR AT
WEYMOUTH, DORSET
RIGHT: SURFER AT
PORTMEOR BEACH, ST
IVES, CORNWALL

ABOVE: SAND SURFER AT
WESTON SUPER MARE

25

Godrevy Head
Cornwall
4 miles (6km) west of Camborne

DON'T MISS

GODREVY LIGHTHOUSE

HELL'S MOUTH

DEADMAN'S COVE

GODREVY ISLAND WITH ITS OCTAGONAL LIGHTHOUSE LIES ¼ MILE (400M) OFFSHORE.

The National Trust property of Godrevy Head stands at the eastern end of St Ives Bay and is the first of a sequence of high rugged cliffs of dark slate that runs uninterrupted to the northeast. Offshore from the headland stands Godrevy Island and its crowning lighthouse. There is ample parking at Godrevy Head on grassy downs that are reached along a winding road. Paths lead across and around the headland, from which inquisitive grey seals can be seen in the offshore waters. To the south lies Gwithian Beach and inland is the village of Gwithian, where there is a handsome church and an attractive pub.

Just east of Godrevy Head and close to the B3301 is the awesome Hell's Mouth, a vast gulf in the cliff where wind and waves continue steadily to erode the softer sedimentary rocks of a faultline. The view is unnerving but is conveniently enjoyed because it is close to the road. Still further east of Godrevy Head lies Deadman's Cove, another gruesomely named venue.

Hayle
Cornwall
3 miles (5km) southeast of St Ives

WINDSWEPT SAND
DUNES PROVIDE A
DRAMATIC BACKDROP
TO HAYLE'S BEACHES.

Victorian tin and copper mining, reflected in such local names as Copperhouse and Foundry, sustained Hayle's industrial past. Today, Hayle's rather straggling extent and its historical decline have denied it picturesque appeal; but awareness of the town's industrial past makes a rewarding visit for those looking for the history under its skin. A walk along the eastern side of the harbour and along the northern side of the large tidal pond of Copperhouse Pool, though not entirely scenic, is worthwhile. The sharp contrast between the dereliction of Hayle's harbour area and the spaciousness and brightness of the beaches in its vicinity is startling.

Access to several miles of beach can be gained from Hayle by following the road through the village of Phillack and out to a car park amidst shoals of chalets. The town has good shops, galleries and craft shops, restaurants and several down-to-earth pubs.

Hayle Estuary is an important winter feeding-ground for wild birds, a bonus to birdwatchers in spring and autumn especially. Some very rare sightings are possible during autumn migrations, when vagrant species from America may be pushed off their north–south migratory path and driven across the Atlantic to Cornwall. The best site is at Lelant Saltings to the west of Hayle. Access is from just off the A30 on the Penzance and St Ives road by the Old Quay House Inn.

St Ives
Cornwall
7 miles (12km) northeast of Penzance

ST IVES' SPECTACULAR WAVES HAVE MADE THE PRETTY TOWN A MECCA FOR SURFERS.

St Ives' rare character springs from its fishing traditions, its artistic inheritance and its tourism industry. There is a clash of style amongst all three at times, but St Ives has survived such competing interests. Not only is the town the archetypal Cornish fishing port but its magnificent beaches of silken sand offer safe family bathing and excellent surf. The town has aimed determinedly upmarket in recent years and has benefited greatly from the Tate St Ives, which opened in 1993. The gallery stands above the spectacular Porthmeor Beach, its curves and crests as white as the waves below. The paintings on display were inspired by local landscapes and are by leading contemporaries of the St Ives School, including Patrick Heron, Peter Lanyon and Terry Frost. The view seaward from the gallery's roof terrace is spectacular. Before the Tate opened, the Barbara Hepworth Museum and Sculpture Garden was the most important artistic attraction here and it remains popular.

St Ives is a delight overall because of its narrow, canyon-like streets, granite cobbles and clear, sea-mirrored light. The parish church of St Ia is one of the finest in Cornwall. The harbour area, known locally as 'Downlong', is a maze of exquisite vernacular granite buildings.

LEFT: FISHING BOATS AND CREWS LINED UP ALONG THE BEACH AT ST IVES.

BELOW: THE TATE GALLERY; THE LONG STRETCH OF SANDY BEACH AT ST IVES.

Land's End
Cornwall
8 miles (13km) southwest of Penzance

The symbolic geography of Land's End demands a visit, although the natural attractions of the area are perhaps best enjoyed outside the busiest holiday periods. Do not expect to find yourselves romantically alone during daylight hours – except in a Force 9 gale. But while rugged weather may enhance the Land's End experience for the true romantic, the venue's numerous covered attractions are enjoyable as wet-weather alternatives. They include exhibitions, gift shops, craft centres and galleries and the Last Labyrinth electronic theatre, where the real experiences of the Cornish coast are cleverly, if sometimes ironically, simulated. There is a choice of eating places within the complex and the Land's End Hotel is in a splendid position overlooking the Longships Lighthouse. There may be queues of traffic on the approach on popular Bank Holidays and during peak holiday periods.

For those who prefer a more robust approach than by car, the coastal path can be followed to Land's End from Sennen in the north (1 mile/1.5km) or from Porthgwarra in the southeast (3 miles/5km).

END-TO-ENDERS
The long walk from John O' Groats, at the northern tip of Scotland, to Land's End has attracted a multitude of people eager to cover the 603 miles (970km) in one trip. Famous End-to-Enders include Ian Botham and Jimmy Saville. Some began anonymously and then became famous, like the round-the-world walker Ffyona Campbell. Most make the trip for personal reasons, or for charities, which have benefited hugely from such efforts. There is an official End-to-Enders Club. Straightforward walking remains the obvious challenge but there have been numerous variations, from four wheels, two wheels and bed-pushes, to nude cyclists (but only for the last sunny Cornish miles). A few determined souls have done it via the coast.

From Land's End the towering cliffs run southeast to Gwennap Head. There they turn eastwards in a succession of surf-tossed coves and commanding headlands, echoing to the rumble of the sea and the cries of gulls.

In a fabulous setting on the western headland is the open-air Minack Theatre, an amphitheatre 150ft (50m) built in 1932 in the style of a classical Greek theatre.

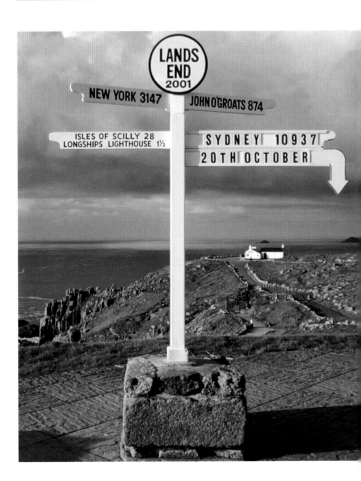

Southwest England

DON'T MISS

THE MINACK THEATRE

SENNEN COVE

LAST LABYRINTH
ELECTRONIC THEATRE

SPECTACULAR CLIFFS
TOWER ABOVE THE
RESTLESS OCEAN AT
LAND'S END.

A SIGNPOST TO
FARAWAY PLACES IS
INEVITABLE AT BRITAIN'S
MOST WESTERLY POINT.

Marazion

Cornwall

3 miles (5km) east of Penzance

DON'T MISS

ST MICHAEL'S MOUNT

PRUSSIA COVE

Marazion was the main trading port of Mount's Bay until an upstart Penzance developed its own markets and port during the 16th century. But Marazion has remained as distinctive as its lovely name, which derives, rather plainly, from the Cornish word for market. There is an informative little museum at the town hall in Market Square and there are antique and craft shops, pleasant pubs, restaurants and cafés.

Marazion Beach offers safe bathing and is a sun trap. It has a reputation for good windsurfing, especially during spring and autumn, when conditions are breezy. The quiet village of Perranuthnoe, a short distance southeast with a south-facing beach, also provides reasonable surfing at times. A few miles further east lies Prussia Cove, a secluded rocky inlet of great charm reached most rewardingly by a 2-mile (3-km) walk along the coast path.

The great complement to Marazion is the castellated St Michael's Mount, the most romantic offshore island in Britain and a matching image to Mont St Michel off the Normandy coast. Fifth-century fishermen dedicated the Mount to

THE 'PART-TIME' ISLAND OF ST MICHAEL'S MOUNT IS CROWNED BY A FAIRYTALE CASTLE.

THE CAUSEWAY AT MARAZION PRESENTS A COBBLED PATH ALONG THE SEASHORE.

St Michael after claims of miraculous sightings of the saint. Even today shafts of celestial light seem drawn to St Michael's Mount, although a view of angels is perhaps less likely. In its day the Mount has been monastery, prison and castle-under-siege. The Mount is nicely defined as a part-time island by successive high tides, during which it may be reached by a pleasant boat trip. At low tide the approach is on foot along a fine cobbled causeway.

The Lizard
Cornwall
Peninsula, southeast of Helston

The tip of the Lizard Peninsula, with its guardian lighthouse, is the furthest south you can go in England. Along the coast, cliffs rising to 200ft (60m) are broken by little rocky coves, with here and there a tiny fishing village and harbour. The Lizard is known for its unique serpentine rock, predominantly green in colour. Serpentine ornaments became fashionable in Victorian times and are still made here as souvenirs. Soapstone was also extracted here. The church at Landewednack has a pulpit and lectern made of the curious stone. Much of the coast is cared for by the National Trust, including Mullion Cove, with its charming old harbour and island bird sanctuary, and Kynance Cove, a popular beauty spot known for its serpentine cliffs, caves and rock formations, where the sea spouts and hisses through a fissure called the Devil's Bellows.

On the eastern side of the peninsula are the simple, white-washed cottages of Cadgwith and Coverack, the latter a celebrated smugglers' haven whose name is Cornish for hideaway. Offshore lie the dreaded reefs of the Manacles, which have torn the life out of many a proud ship. Drowned seamen sleep their last sleep in the churchyard at St Keverne, whose tall spire was a vital landmark for ships in the Channel.

THE LIZARD HAS AN IMPRESSIVE COASTLINE OF BLACK CLIFFS AND HIDDEN COVES.

Helford

Cornwall

16 miles (24km) southwest of Truro

ROMANTIC, TREE-LINED
FRENCHMAN'S CREEK
HAS SEVERAL LITERARY
ASSOCIATIONS.

DON'T MISS

GLENDURGAN GARDEN
(NATIONAL TRUST)

TREBAH GARDEN

SLEEPY HELFORD IS
PROBABLY THE MORE
SERENE FACE OF
MARITIME CORNWALL.

There is irresistible romance attached to Helford and its tree-shrouded river and creeks. The price is that the area can become uncomfortably busy during popular holiday periods. But the dense nature of this serene landscape rewards those who explore further than Helford itself, lovely though the village is. The countryside is gentle, compared with the extremes of the coast, and although access along the riverbank is limited in places, there are a number of fine walks to be enjoyed from Helford.

Just to the west lies the famous Frenchman's Creek, romanticised by the novelists Sir Arthur Quiller-Couch and Daphne du Maurier and still enchanting today, even when the falling tide reveals an expanse of mud. A path leads east from Helford to the coast at Dennis Head and to St Anthony and Gillan. These quiet places are best visited on foot; parking is difficult and is not encouraged.

A seasonal passenger ferry from Helford sails to Helford Passage on the north bank, from where the Glendurgan Garden and the adjacent Trebah Garden can be visited. Glendurgan is one of the great sub-tropical gardens of the Southwest, situated on the banks of the Helford River near Mawnan Smith. Rhododendrons, camellias and hydrangeas flourish amidst lovely woodland and there is an engaging maze. Among the many attractions of Trebah Garden is a fine water garden. The smaller garden at Penjerrick, which is just over a mile north of Mawnan Smith, is home to a flourishing and vibrant collection of Chilean firebushes, magnolias and azaleas.

Falmouth
Cornwall
12 miles (19km) south of Truro

DON'T MISS

PENDENNIS CASTLE

NATIONAL MARITIME
MUSEUM CORNWALL

THIS RESTFUL SCENE BELIES FALMOUTH'S BUSTLING LIFE, BOTH PAST AND PRESENT.

Vessels of all types and sizes still bustle in and out of Falmouth, lending excitement and atmosphere to one of the world's largest natural harbours. Falmouth developed as a port after Henry VIII built Pendennis and St Mawes castles, the guardians of the Fal Estuary. Both are built in the distinctive clover-leaf design, and St Mawes is particularly renowned as a fine example of military architecture, with its dungeons, barrack rooms and cannon-lined castle walls.

During the late 17th century the port became a packet station, from where small, fast-sailing brigantines took mail to northwest Spain, and later to North America, the West Indies and South America. Gold and silver bullion was carried and the packets provided a passenger service. By 1850 a vigorous pilchard fishery, the development of Falmouth docks and a thriving shipbuilding industry secured Falmouth's position as a major port, which is still busy today.

Falmouth's rather straggling form gives it less unity that might be expected of a port, as the town follows the riverside through a chain of linking main streets, but this makes it intriguing to explore.

Fowey

Cornwall

7 miles (11km) south of Lostwithiel

The steep, narrow streets of this pleasant old town plunge down the hillside above a lovely, yacht-crowded haven on the estuary of the River Fowey. Blessed with one of the best natural harbours on the south coast, Fowey (the name is pronounced to rhyme with 'toy') was an important port in the Middle Ages, on the trade route between the mainland Europe and Ireland that crossed Cornwall overland to the Camel Estuary. Its piratical seamen, the 'Fowey Gallants', were not averse to preying on ships in the English Channel and even raiding the French coast, sometimes provoking fierce retaliation – the French came and burned the town down in 1457. In the 19th century local ships traded to the Mediterranean and across the Atlantic, and Fowey became a china clay port. The parish church of St Fimbarrus has some fine monuments to the Rashleigh family, whose 15th-century town house is now the Ship Inn. The Lugger Inn is a 17th-century hostelry, the town hall in Trafalgar Square – now housing a museum – dates from the 1790s, and there are many other interesting old buildings.

MANDERLEY

The wealthy merchant dynasty of Rashleigh had their country house just outside Fowey at Menabilly. It was later for many years the home of Daphne du Maurier, who dearly loved this part of Cornwall and included it in many of her novels and adventure stories. Menabilly itself was the inspiration for the famous 'Manderley' of *Rebecca,* and also appears in *The King's General.*

DON'T MISS

ST CATHERINE'S CASTLE

ST FINBARRUS' CHURCH

FOWEY'S JOSTLING HOUSES LOOK OUT OVER THE RIVER'S PEACEFUL ESTUARY.

Polperro

Cornwall

3 miles (5km) southwest of Looe

Polperro rambles delightfully down to the sea. The pattern of narrow lanes and alleyways and steep flanking streets is set by the enclosing walls of the wooded valley within which Polperro lies, and is more engaging than in any other Cornish village. The inner harbour sits squarely amidst houses and the boisterous stream, known as the Rafiel, pours into it beneath a Saxon bridge and beside the delightful House on the Props, with its rough wooden supports. When the sun shines, Polperro flickers with light and shade. Polperro was always a fishing village and remains so today, though its charm has made it one of the most visited places in Cornwall. Access to Polperro is on foot from a car park at Crumplehorn above the main village. This quaint village is an attractive place to while away some time, with its numerous shops, art and craft galleries, pubs and restaurants.

Plymouth
Devon
43 miles (69km) southwest of Exeter

DON'T MISS

CITY MUSEUM & ART GALLERY

NATIONAL MARITIME MUSEUM

MERCHANT'S HOUSE MUSEUM

PLYMOUTH DOME

ROYAL CITADEL

A STATUE OF SIR FRANCIS DRAKE STANDS PROUDLY ON PLYMOUTH HOE OVERLOOKING THE BUSY MARINA.

Busy today with warships, cross-Channel ferries, cargo boats, fishing smacks, yachts and small craft, Plymouth Sound is a magnificent natural harbour of some 4,500 acres (1,800ha), formed by the junction of the rivers Tamar and Plym. An inlet to the northeast, Sutton Harbour, was the original port, and the Royal Citadel, a fortress with walls up to 70ft (23m) high, was built to protect it in the 1660s. The Royal Naval Dockyard in the Hamoaze (the Tamar Estuary) was opened in 1691. Since the 1840s a colossal mile-long (1.5km) breakwater in the middle of the Sound, designed by John Rennie, has protected it all.

Plymouth is one of Britain's great seafaring towns, with a history of maritime enterprise and adventure going far back into the Middle Ages. Armies were shipped over to France from here in the 14th and 15th centuries. The formidable Elizabethan seadogs – Drake, Hawkins, Frobisher, Gilbert and Raleigh – all set out from Plymouth on their adventures. Sir Francis Drake sailed from here in 1577 to voyage round the world and, in 1588, after calmly finishing his game of bowls on the Hoe, he sailed out of the Sound to give the Spanish Armada a drubbing. In 1772, Captain Cook set off from Plymouth in the *Resolution* to sail round the world.

Targeted as a major naval base, the centre of Plymouth was heavily bombed and severely damaged in World War II, and was rebuilt during a period of singularly undistinguished architecture. The narrow streets of the Barbican area close to Sutton Harbour, however, with the fish quay and a bustling market, have retained their old character and

atmosphere, and several of the merchants' and ship captains' houses of Tudor times are open to the public. The Mayflower Stone and Steps here commemorate the Pilgrim Fathers, who left Plymouth for the New World in the *Mayflower*, in 1620.

Slapton Sands
Devon
5 miles (8km) southwest of Dartmouth

SLAPTON LEY IS AN IMPORTANT WILDLIFE RESERVE, RICH IN FISH AND BIRD LIFE.

The sea has piled up a long, straight bar of shingle that stretches for five or six miles (8–9.5km) along the coast north of Start Point. The A379 road from Kingsbridge to Dartmouth runs along the shore over Slapton Sands, which are actually shingle, although there is some sand here at low tide.

On the beach grow such plants as sea radish and shore dock, and a monument recalls that this part of the South Hams area of South Devon was taken over as a rehearsal ground for American troops for the D-Day landings in 1944. Several villages were temporarily evacuated so that the soldiers could train for the Normandy beaches.

Behind and sheltered by the shingle ridge is the freshwater lagoon of Slapton Ley, a mile (1.5km) or so long, up to 10ft (3m) deep and covering about 270 acres (110ha). It is a nature reserve rich in fish and plant life. The northern end is thick with reeds and willow. Great crested grebe, stonechat, goldcrest, coot and mallard breed here, migrant birds rest here in spring and autumn, and in winter huge flocks of gulls gather on the beach and the Ley.

Brixham

Devon

5 miles (8km) south of Torquay

DON'T MISS

BRIXHAM HERITAGE FESTIVAL (MAY)

SIR FRANCIS DRAKE'S *GOLDEN HIND*

BRIXHAM MUSEUM

BRIXHAM BOASTS A FULL-SIZE REPLICA OF SIR FRANCIS DRAKE'S SHIP, *GOLDEN HIND*.

Torbay, or the English Riviera, is one of the West Country's leading tourist honeypots. At the southern end of the bay, the picturesque harbour and the steep, narrow streets of Brixham lie sheltered in the lee of Berry Head. In 1850 the town claimed to be England's leading fishing port, with more than 270 vessels – brigs, schooners and smacks – amounting to 20,000 tons of shipping. The town still has a fishing fleet, but a much smaller one. At the harbour's edge a statue of William of Orange commemorates his arrival here in 1688 on his way to be proclaimed King William III at Newton Abbot – and later in London. Nearby, a full-size replica of Sir Francis Drake's *Golden Hind*, the ship in which he sailed round the world, is moored close to the old market house. The local history is expounded in Brixham Museum, which has a special section on the coastguard service. A monument in All Saints' churchyard recalls 100 sailors who drowned in a terrible storm in 1866, when many boats were driven on to the rocks.

Torquay

Devon

18 miles (30km) south of Exeter

Torquay is south Devon at its most Mediterranean – a balmy climate, palm trees bathed in coloured lights and millionaires' yachts basking in the marina. Yet this is also the capital of the English Riviera and the birthplace of Agatha Christie, the much-loved crime writer.

From humble beginnings as a fishing village, the town's resort career began during Napoleonic times, and by the Victorian era its mild winters were attracting people with consumption and fashionable visitors on doctors' orders. By 1850 it was proclaiming itself 'Queen of the Watering Holes', and today it is the country's second most popular seaside resort after Blackpool.

In the centre of town is the lively marina and harbour, including the listed copper-domed Edwardian Pavilion which now houses an excellent shopping centre. Eastwards the cliffs rise up to Daddy Hole Plain, a great chasm in the cliff where the plain meets the sea, and the views from here are superb. Continue east to the point at Hope's Nose for more sea panoramas.

The beaches are numerous and well spread apart. The most attractive of the major beaches is Oddicombe, with its picturesque backdrop of steep sandstone cliffs topped by lush woodland. The Oddicombe/Babbacombe area is also home to Torquay's best tourist attractions, including Kents Cavern. As far as we know, the earliest human occupation of Britain was about 400,000 years ago and Kent's Cavern is one of only two sites in the country that provide evidence for this (the other is a quarry in Somerset).

THE CAPITAL OF THE ENGLISH RIVIERA HAS A DISTINCTLY MEDITERRANEAN FEEL.

TORQUAY IS SECOND ONLY TO BLACKPOOL AS BRITAIN'S MOST POPULAR SEASIDE SPOT.

DON'T MISS

LIVING COASTS

KENT'S CAVERN

BABBACOMBE MODEL VILLAGE

BYGONES EXHIBITION

TORRE ABBEY HISTORIC HOUSE & GARDENS

Sidmouth

Devon

13 miles (21km) east of Exeter

Dignified, charming and sedate, like a smaller and quieter Brighton, the town of Sidmouth decorously occupies a gap in the great red cliffs along the coast east of Exmouth. It is set at the point where the River Sid, after struggling for miles to reach the sea, is baulked just short of its objective by a bulky bank of shingle and seems to come despondently to a halt.

The town, once a fishing village, developed as a seaside resort in the Regency period, when the rich and fashionable built themselves substantial 'cottages' here. It is a place of shining white terraces, elegant wrought-iron balconies with tent-shaped canopies, and flower-packed gardens nurtured by the gentle climate, with some fine specimens of early Gothic Revival architecture and the fashion for the thatched and wildly picturesque cottage. Examples include the Strawberry Hill Gothic and castellated battlements of Coburg Terrace, the insanely bargeboarded Woodlands Hotel of 1815, and Beach House on the front, with its Gothic Revival windows and delicate ironwork. Indeed, Sidmouth claims to have England's most beautiful council house – Pauntley Cottage, with its domed roof of thatch, pointed windows and charming cottage garden.

ABOVE: DECKCHAIRS AND HOLIDAYMAKERS ON SIDMOUTH'S ESPLANADE, WHICH WAS BUILT IN 1837.

WALKERS ON THE HILLS ABOVE SIDMOUTH ENJOY A VIEW OF THE STRIKING RED SANDSTONE CLIFFS.

Beer

Devon

1 mile (1.5km) west of Seaton

DON'T MISS

PECORAMA PLEASURE
GARDENS

BEER QUARRY CAVES

BEER HAS BRIGHT CHALK CLIFFS, UNLIKE THE RED SANDSTONE OF ITS NEIGHBOURS.

The lovely little fishing village of Beer is in one of the most sheltered positions along this coast, and its fishermen gained a reputation for hardy seamanship because they could put to sea when others were kept at home by the pounding waves. Beer also has the most westerly chalk cliffs in England, contrasting vividly with the deep red cliffs nearby and the lush green of the surrounding countryside. It once had a renowned lace-making industry, established here by refugees from the Netherlands, and the quality of the work rivalled the more famous Honiton lace. Beer lace was used to decorate Queen Victoria's wedding dress.

To the west of the village are the Pecorama Pleasure Gardens, set high on a hillside overlooking the village and coastline. Apart from the beautiful gardens, there is a miniature steam and diesel passenger railway that offers some of the best views across Lyme Bay.

The Beer Quarry Caves offer a totally different experience, with an hour-long tour of these man-made caverns, which extend for a quarter of a mile (0.4km) in each direction. The Romans worked the quarries nearly 2,000 years ago, and the vast caverns with vaulted roofs and natural stone pillars were hewn by hand down the centuries.

Chesil Beach
Dorset
8 miles (13km) northwest of Weymouth

DON'T MISS

ABBOTSBURY SWANNERY

In Old English 'chesil' means shingle, but this curious natural phenomenon is no ordinary shingle beach. It comprises a 17-mile (27km) bank of pebbles up to 35ft (11m) high and 450–600ft (137–183m) wide, enclosing the Fleet Lagoon. The stones are naturally graded by powerful currents (swimming here is highly dangerous) and decrease from cannonball-sized in the east to pea-sized in the west. The best view is from above, on Portland.

In the nearby village of Abbotsbury, thatched cottages line the streets of this village, while beyond a 15th-century tithe barn and the hilltop St Catherine's Chapel of c1400 are tangible reminders of the Benedictine abbey, founded in 1026, that gave the village its name. Built in the 15th century to store one-tenth of all local produce that was harvested, the abbey is now a children's themed play area.

Abbotsbury Swannery, set up by monks in the 14th century, gives unrivalled opportunities to see swans close up. Nest-building occurs between March and the end of April, hatching is mid-May to the end of June, and cygnets gain their wings in early autumn. There are feeding sessions daily.

Lyme Regis to Dragon's Hill

A walk in the hills behind the town that ends on the famous Cobb.

What to look for In 1811, in the cliffs near the town, Mary Anning discovered the first complete icthyosaurus – a marine reptile a bit like a dolphin, which grew up to 33ft (10m) long. Dinosaurland is a fascinating fossil museum, with icthyosaurs, plesiosaurs and other Jurassic delights, plus a time gallery to show what life was like 4.6 billion years ago. Take your own finds to its fossil clinic, or go with an expert on a fossil walk.

While you're there For something different, go to sea. Deep-sea fishing trips are offered from Lyme and there are lots of little boats available for charter. They advertise a variety of adventures and expeditions on the seafront near the Cobb. There's mackerel fishing in season, too.

ALTHOUGH BUSY IN THE SUMMER SEASON, THE BEACHES ARE RARELY CROWDED.

THE SHELTERED HARBOUR OF LYME REGIS WAS ONCE DORSET'S SECOND LARGEST PORT.

LYME REGIS IS STILL AN ACTIVE FISHING PORT.

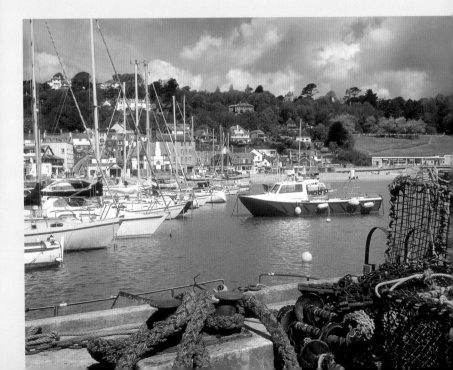

Along the famous breakwater at Lyme

❶ From the harbour car park, face inland and take the path to the left of the bowling green, up some steps between wooden chalets, signed 'Coastal Path'. Cross a road and continue via more steps up through steep woodland, beside a stream. Cross a stile at the top and turn right. Go through a gate and continue along a path and then a road between villas, to cross a car park. Cross the road ahead and, with Coram Tower on your left, go straight on down Pound Road. Pass the thatched Cursbrook Hotel. Meet the B3165 opposite the Mariners Hotel. Cross this then go down Woodmead Road. Soon turn left through a gate and follow the path down through a plantation.

❷ Go through a gate on to Roman Road. Bear right, cross the River Lim and turn left down a lane. By Middle Mill Farm cross a footbridge. Continue along the valley floor. At the corner bear right through a gate, cross a footbridge and bear right at the fork. Pass a thatched cottage on the left and turn right over a bridge (blue marker). Follow this path through woods to a gate. Continue past the sewage works and through another gate into a field.

❸ Go straight on up the hill, with Sleech Wood to your left. Continue through a gate. Near the top of Dragon's Hill go through a gate and turn right, down a lane. Stay on this below a caravan park to emerge on Charmouth Road. Turn right and follow this for 1/2 mile (800m), down into the town, taking care where the pavement runs out. Pass the former London pub (now a B & B) and enter the old town. Turn right into Monmouth Street, passing through a delightful square with gardens. Keep right, up the hill, towards Dinosaurland. Pass Dinosaurland on the right, with a fossil museum and shop. Continue uphill. Take the riverside path on the left, signposted 'Town Mill'. The stream is on your left, the river below to your right.

❹ Turn left up Mill Lane, and right on to Coombe Street, towards the harbour. Here you get the impression of lots of tiny houses tightly packed together. Bear left at the end, by the Lyme Fossil Shop, on to Broad Street, towards the tourist information centre. Turn right by the Guildhall, and right again along the sea via Guncliffe Walk, really a disguise for a new sewage scheme.

❺ Pass a huge anchor and bear right up Broad Street, as far as the Royal Lion Hotel. Walk down the opposite pavement, around the old shambles, to Bell Cliff. Go down the steps and turn right along Marine Parade. Local philanthropist Thomas Hollis created this walkway in 1771 as an alternative to the lower cart road. Shingle on your left gives way to sand near the amusement arcades. The buildings on the eastern arm of the harbour now

house an aquarium. Continue up a lane, passing the Royal Standard on your left. Bear left by the Cobb Arms and walk to the end of the Cobb.

❻ The Cobb is a breakwater, first constructed in the 13th century to protect the town from the sea. The sheltered harbour it created made Lyme Dorset's second largest port. The Cobb was rebuilt in Portland

stone in the early 19th century with a walkway on the sheltered side. While the shipping trade had waned by then, cargoes were still being unloaded here into the 20th century. Jane Austen visited Lyme Regis in 1804, and set a pivotal scene of her novel *Persuasion* (1818) on the Cobb – the impetuous Louisa Musgrove mistimed her jump from the steps. (The house where Jane Austen stayed was recently pulled down and replaced by a memorial garden, above Marine Parade.) The Cobb gained contemporary fame when scenes for the 1981 film, *The French Lieutenant's Woman*, were shot here. The film was based on the novel by John Fowles, who was curator of the local history museum for many years.

❼ Turning left by the Lifeboat Station to return to the car park.

Distance: 4 miles (6.5km)

Time: 2hrs Climb: 427ft (130m)

Terrain: Town centre, promenade, woodland steps, paths, 1 stile. Town, cliffs and hinterland of steep valley.

OS Map: aqua3 OS Explorer 116 Lyme Regis & Bridport

Grid reference: SY 337916

Dogs: Very busy in summer; dogs banned from shingle beach.

Parking: Pay-and-display near Cobb (other car parks on route) signposted at several car parks and seafront.

Weymouth

Dorset

26 miles (42km) west of Bournemouth

DON'T MISS

NOTHE FORT

SEA LIFE PARK **&** RSPB NATURE RESERVE

BREWERS QUAY

Once George III (1738–1820) began visiting this Dorset seaside town in 1789, it soon became a fashionable holiday place. Much of the original character of the town has been retained in its Georgian façades, ironwork balconies and bow windows.

The long arc of golden sand, which offers safe bathing in the sheltered bay, hosts numerous traditional attractions such as Punch and Judy puppet shows. The harbour is overlooked by Brewers Quay, a brewery converted into courtyards and cobbled alleys with attractions and specialist shops. In Barrack Road, Nothe Fort is a huge Victorian fort with coastal views and 70 rooms to explore.

A 15-minute walk (or a train ride from the Esplanade) east along the seafront leads to Lodmoor Country Park. It includes an RSPB reserve and the Sea Life Park aquarium.

THE HARBOUR IS A STARTING POINT FOR BOAT TRIPS, AS WELL AS FERRIES TO THE CHANNEL ISLANDS.

THE WIDE, SHELTERED BAY AT WEYMOUTH MAKES THE TOWN A POPULAR AND SAFE HOLIDAY RESORT.

Lulworth Cove
Dorset
5 miles (8km) south of Wool

DON'T MISS

DURDLE DOOR

LULWORTH HERITAGE CENTRE

KIMMERIDGE BAY

LULWORTH COVE IS A REMARKABLE FEATURE OF DORSET AND A WORLD HERITAGE SITE.

On the Purbeck Heritage Coast between Swanage and Weymouth, Lulworth Cove is part of an astounding coastline with numerous geological oddities, such as a natural arch, the remains of a fossil forest just below the cliffs and strange natural shapes.

The cove itself is an oval bay displaying textbook cross-sections of spectacularly folded rock strata. A 1-mile (1.5-km) walk west along the well-worn (and steep) track from the car park leads to the natural limestone arch of Durdle Door, above a long, clean and (mostly) pebbly beach. Close to the west side of the cove the waves foam into Stair Hole, another natural sculpture. Here the earth's forces have lifted, twisted and folded the rock strata over 90 degrees. The cliffs present a risk of falling rocks and the foot of it should be treated with great caution – public notices warn of the dangers of climbing on the rocks.

LULWORTH COVE IS A
NATURAL HORSE-SHOE
SHAPED HARBOUR
FORMED ABOUT
10,000 YEARS AGO.

The wide range of habitats resulting from this geological diversity supports a variety of birdlife: kittiwakes, shags, cormorants and fulmars on the cliffs, along with buzzards, kestrels and occasional peregrines. Lulworth has its own butterfly, the Lulworth Skipper, first discovered in 1832. This small brown-and-black species is seen in July and August and is very rare outside Dorset. Among the variety of colourful wild flowers found here are five rare species of orchid.

At certain times you are allowed into the Lulworth Army Ranges. This coastal strip extends east to Kimmeridge over some of the wildest scenery on the south coast. Walking is tough, with steep gradients and dizzying drops, and you must keep to the paths at all times as there are unexploded munitions lying around.

Boat trips give unrivalled views of this dramatic coastline. The Heritage Centre has informative videos and displays and the modern Rock Gallery tells the story of Lulworth from 150 million years ago to the present day.

ABOVE: THE FOSSIL
FOREST CONTAINS THE
REMAINS AND MOULDS
OF LATE JURASSIC OR
EARLY CRETACEOUS
CONIFEROUS TREES.

Portsmouth

Hampshire

65 miles (105km) southwest of London

DON'T MISS

HISTORIC YARD AND HMS VICTORY

CHARLES DICKENS' BIRTHPLACE MUSEUM

SOUTHSEA CASTLE

HMS *WARRIOR* IS THE WORLD' FIRST IRON-CLAD BATTLESHIP.

Portsmouth is the home of Britain's naval heritage, with fabulous historic ships and boat tours. It sprawls inelegantly on and around its island site, and at first sight may not seem the place for a day out. But it has pockets of huge historic interest, mostly concentrated around the waterfront. It has been a naval base since the 12th century and the centre of one of the most powerful seaborne fighting forces in history. The city is the home port of the Royal Navy and was heavily bombed during World War II.

A couple of minutes' walk from Portsmouth Harbour station is the Historic Dockyard with its celebrated warships. Naval officers guide you round Nelson's flagship HMS *Victory* to recall the appalling conditions on board and show the spot where Nelson died in battle in 1805. Close by is the world's first iron-clad battleship, HMS *Warrior*, launched in 1860. Rescued in 1982 after sinking in 1545, Henry VIII's warship the *Mary Rose* is constantly sprayed to prevent its timbers from disintegrating; the rich array of finds from the wreck is on display. The Royal Naval Museum charts the history of British maritime defence.

For 2000, Portsmouth tidied up its waterside with an ambitious development called Gunwharf Quays, a mix of designer shopping, entertainment, and eating and drinking places, plus the venue for international maritime events. At the end of the High Street lies Old Portsmouth, an area of cobbled streets lined with Tudor and Georgian houses and pubs. Named Spice Island at the height of the spice trade, press gangs once roamed these streets seeking new naval recruits, whom they forced to join a leaving ship.

Portsmouth's first harbour, the Camber, is still a working dock. The Round Tower and Square Tower have guarded the entrance to the harbour for 500 years. You can also take a 45-minute cruise from the Historic Dockyard to see modern warships; or sail out to Spitbank Fort.

At Southsea, backed by wide lawns, municipal gardens and Victorian villas, there is a shingle beach. Southsea Castle, on Clarence Esplanade, was built in 1595 to protect Portsmouth against French invasion, and was only withdrawn from active service in 1960. The D-Day Museum is next door.

Isle of Wight
Isle of Wight

The combination of sandy beaches and chalk cliffs topped by grassy downs helped to make the Isle of Wight a magnet to visitors in the 19th century. Among them were Queen Victoria, Prince Albert and their children, who had a summer holiday home near Cowes at Osborne House. Their presence helped to draw the middle classes to the island, and the house was full of happy memories for the old queen when she died there in 1901.

Though the island measures only 23 miles (37km) one way and 13 (21km) the other, it has a surprising variety of scenery. At the extreme western tip, the Needles are pointed stacks of white chalk, surveyed cautiously from the mainland by the Needles Old Battery, built in 1862 against the French. Nearby Alum Bay is known for its multi-coloured cliffs. There are said to be 12 different colours and shades of sand here (the main ones are yellow-brown, white, black, green and red) and they are used in souvenirs. To the east lies Tennyson Down, where the poet liked to stroll, and the chalk cliffs of Freshwater Bay. The southwestern coast is cut by a succession of deep chasms, or chines, penetrating inland – the best known and most commercialised of them is Blackgang Chine.

DON'T MISS

THE NEEDLES PARK

BEMBRIDGE WINDMILL

CARISBROOKE CASTLE

OSBORNE HOUSE

ISLE OF WIGHT STEAM RAILWAY

THE LANDMARK WHITE SHARP-TIPPED NEEDLES WERE ONCE FIRMLY CONNECTED TO THE MAINLAND.

A major factor in the 19th-century development of Wight tourism was the belief that the air and climate were good for invalids, and especially consumptives. The island's senior resort is sheltered Ventnor on the southeast coast, which at one time was officially declared to be the healthiest place in England. The sea wall and esplanade were built in 1848 and eager developers piled Victorian Gothic and seaside Swiss-style houses on the steep rock terraces of the Undercliff, with the front doors in one street lying level with the chimneys of another. A little to the north, Shanklin is another cliff-hanging Victorian and Edwardian resort, with a sandy beach that runs on to the amusements and mile-long (1.5km) esplanade of Sandown. Ryde, where the Portsmouth ferries arrive, is also popular with holidaymakers.

Early August regularly brings Wight into the news as the yacht-racing season peaks at Cowes, where the Royal Yacht Squadron commands the harbour with a battery of miniature brass cannon. There is a good maritime museum here, and another at Bembridge, which has a fine natural harbour. Along the northwest coast, yachts and small craft proliferate among the narrow creeks.

Many eminent Victorians were drawn to the Isle of Wight, among them Alfred, Lord Tennyson, who had a house called Farringford there from the 1850s. He loved to stargaze through a telescope on his roof, walk on the down – which is now named after him – and contemplate the geology of Alum Bay. He wrote 'The Charge of the Light Brigade', and much of 'Idylls of the King' there, entertained numerous distinguished visitors, and was made to pose for photographs by Julia Margaret Cameron, who lived at Dimbola nearby. In 1888, after one of his last trips to the island on the Yarmouth ferry, he wrote 'Crossing the Bar'. His granite monument stands on Tennyson Down.

THE ISLE OF WIGHT HAS BEEN A POPULAR SEASIDE RESORT SINCE THE 19TH CENTURY.

THE EXTENSIVE MARINA AT COWES HOSTS A FAMOUS REGATTA EVERY YEAR.

COMPTON BAY IS ONE
OF THE MOST UNSPOILT
BEACHES ON THE ISLE
OF WIGHT.

Bosham
West Sussex
4 miles (6km) west of Chichester

RED-ROOFED COTTAGES
AND THE SAXON HOLY TRINITY
CHURCH PLAY A MAJOR PART IN
MAKING BOSHAM PICTURESQUE.

LOW TIDE SEES BOATS
BEACHED, WHEREAS
HIGH TIDE FLOODS THE
HARBOUR ROAD.

The *Bayeux Tapestry* shows Harold on his way to mass in Bosham Church before he set out on his unsuccessful voyage to Normandy in 1064. Bosham is also the place where Canute unsuccessfully bid the tide to retreat.

Today, it is a picturesque village with pastel-coloured houses set on the creek in Chichester Harbour with sailing craft everywhere. The High Street is a narrow lane of flint, tile-hung and brick cottages with a little green called Quay Meadow. The road beside the harbour floods at high tide.

Brighton

East Sussex

48 miles (77 km) south of London

In 1753 a certain Dr Richard Russell of Lewes moved to an obscure fishing village named Brighthelmstone on the south coast. He successfully trumpeted the medical virtues of sea air, sea bathing and even drinking sea water, judiciously mixed with milk. He also promoted a mineral spring called St Ann's Well in nearby Hove. From these bracing beginnings developed the splendidly self-indulgent acknowledged queen of British seaside resorts, with its elegant Regency terraces, squares and crescents, its grand Victorian churches, its piers and promenade and aquarium, its smart shops, restaurants and racecourse, its ice-cream parlours and whelk stalls and every variety of seaside amusement, from the raffish to the exquisite.

The most important single visitor in the early days was the Prince Regent, afterwards George IV. He first came here in 1783, later took a house and eventually employed the architect John Nash to build him a stately pleasure-dome, the Royal Pavilion, a wonderful oriental fantasy with dazzling Chinese-style interiors, imitation bamboo everywhere and a kitchen staffed by serried ranks of gleaming copper pans. Brighton's fashionable reputation was made, and the town expanded rapidly – eastwards to Kemp Town and to the west until it bumped into Hove. Hove has its own sumptuous Regency squares and terraces, and an impressive Victorian legacy in the form of a working steam museum of vast hissing machines in a restored pumping station.

BRIGHTON PIER HAS BEEN A PLACE OF ENTERTAINMENT FOR OVER A CENTURY.

DON'T MISS

THE ROYAL PAVILION

THE LANES

PRESTON MANOR

THE MARINA

Beachy Head and the Seven Sisters
East Sussex
3 miles (5km) southeast of Newhaven

THE BEST SEA VIEW ALONG THIS COAST IS FROM THE INFAMOUS BEACHY HEAD.

The high chalk ridge of the South Downs ends at the south coast in spectacular style with a range of dazzling white cliffs at Beachy Head and the Seven Sisters. Useful starting points are from the visitor centre: you can walk out to Cuckmere Haven, the village green at East Dean and Birling Gap, where steps lead to a pebble beach. A path heads along the cliff tops, but keep away from the sheer edge, as the cliff can crumble away without warning.

This area of the Sussex coast is an object lesson in the waywardness of fortune. The River Ouse, which rises inland east of Horsham, flows through Lewes on its way to the sea, and originally reached it at Seaford – though it was given to changing its course through the marshes and shifting shingle banks along the shore. Seaford had a harbour and was a

'limb' or junior partner of the Cinque Port of Hastings. In the 16th century, a group of local landowners decided to drain the marshes and improve the navigation by cutting a canal from the wandering river to the sea at Newhaven – which gained a harbour, prospered and eventually became the ferry port for Dieppe. Seaford was robbed of its harbour and was reduced to insignificance, huddled sadly around its Norman church, until the 1870s, when the Esplanade was built and it began to develop as a decorous seaside resort. On the front is the most westerly of the 19th-century Martello towers, built for coastal defence, which has been turned into a local history museum.

An enjoyable walk leads up over the heights of Seaford Head – a smaller edition of Beachy Head – and through the earthworks of an Iron Age fort to Cuckmere Haven, an old smuggling haven where the meandering River Cuckmere reluctantly enters the sea. Here, contraband goods from France were unloaded. A shingle bank supports sea beet and sea kale, and protects a marshy lagoon where winter wildfowl feed. Beyond Cuckmere Haven lie the Seven Sisters, a tremendous wall of shining chalk, with eight cliffs. At the western end is Haven Brow, and beyond it lie Short Brow, Rough Brow, Brass Point, Flagstaff Point, Flat Hill, Baily's Hill and finally Went Hill Brow. The western cliffs, Cuckmere Haven and the river valley form the Seven Sisters Country Park, which covers some 700 acres (280ha) of cliff, shingle, salt-marsh and downland, rich in plant and animal life. The South Downs Way runs along the top of the cliffs.

THE EIGHT CLIFFS OF THE SEVEN SISTERS BASK IN THE GLOW OF THE EVENING SUN.

THE PEBBLY BEACH AT BIRLING GAP IS POPULAR WITH VISITORS ALL YEAR LONG.

DEATH ON THE CLIFF

In the 18th century Cuckmere Haven was used by a particularly savage gang led by a man named Stanton Collins, whose headquarters were in Alfriston at the Olde Smugglers Inn. In a notorious incident one dark night, the gang moved the lumps of chalk, which the customs officers employed to follow the cliff-top path, so that a revenue man slipped over the edge. He clung on by his fingertips, pleading desperately to be rescued, but the smugglers stamped on his hands and he fell to his death.

Eastbourne

East Sussex

19 miles (31km) east of Brighton

DON'T MISS

WISH TOWER PUPPET MUSEUM

TOWNER ART GALLERY

'HOW WE LIVED THEN' MUSEUM

THE VIEW FROM ONE OF THE THREE LEVELS OF EASTBOURNE'S POPULAR PROMENADE.

Sheltered by the South Downs and the bulk of Beachy Head, Eastbourne basks in an exceptionally high sunshine count and a reputation for restrained middle-class charm.

After centuries of inconspicuous existence it was developed as a resort in the 1850s, principally by the seventh Duke of Devonshire who owned much of it. There were grand hotels, comfortable villas, smart shops and attractive parks. The imposing Grand Parade was laid out along the front and a pier designed by Eugenius Birch.

At the edge of the shingle beach the promenade runs on three levels, with municipal flower gardens along the top. The Redoubt, an early 19th-century fortress, now houses an aquarium and a military museum. Lifeboats from the earliest days to the present are on view in the country's first lifeboat museum, opened here in 1937, and a rewarding array of British art of the 19th and 20th centuries can be found in the Towner Art Gallery, including major works by Eastbourne artist and designer Eric Ravilious.

Hastings

East Sussex

32 miles (51km) east of Brighton

FISHING BOATS ARE DRAWN UP DAILY ON THE SHINGLE AT THE FRONT'S EAST END.

UNIQUE TO HASTINGS ARE THE 'DEELES', TALL HUTS FOR STORING FISHING NETS.

DON'T MISS

OLD TOWN MUSEUM OF LOCAL HISTORY

SMUGGLERS ADVENTURE

1066 STORY IN HASTINGS CASTLE

It was to Hastings that William the Conqueror led his army after landing at Pevensey. The town was already an important port and continued to be, as a leading Cinque Port, until stormy seas blocked the harbour with shingle. Fishing boats are still drawn up on the shingle of the Stade at the eastern end of the front, and the old town lies inland from here, in a narrow valley between the high sandstone cliffs of the West Hill and the East Hill. There's a museum of local history in the old town hall, and the Shipwreck Heritage Centre displays material from important local wrecks. A cliff railway runs up West Hill, to the remains of the Norman castle and the 1066 Story exhibition. The extensive St Clement's Caves, partly natural and partly man-made, are open to visitors as The Smugglers Adventure. Below, the 1820s church of St Mary with its Greek Revival-style portico is being restored.

Modern Hastings developed to the west – on past the Victorian pier – as a seaside resort from the later 18th century on, and neighbouring St Leonard's was laid out by James Burton and his son Decimus in the 1820s and 1830s.

Rye

East Sussex

9 miles (15km) northeast of Hastings

Reposing on its hill above the surrounding levels, Rye is one of England's most beautiful and charming towns. With a wealth of half-timbered and Georgian houses, its winding cobbled streets have frequent turnings that open up freshly pleasing prospects, and its many old inns, smart shops, tea rooms, galleries and potteries give it a thoroughly civilised air. The best approach is from the east, with a romantic view of the town across the marshes.

The sea has receded and left the town high and dry two miles (3km) inland, but Rye was once one of the leading south coast ports. It provided ships for the royal fleet and fish for the royal table. It was frequently raided by the French, who burned most of the town down in 1377 – after which the English government hanged several of the leading citizens for faint-heartedness. The local history is told in the museum in the Ypres Tower, part of the 13th-century defences. The heritage centre has a fine model of the town.

On top of the hill, Rye's crowning glory is the Norman church of St Mary, with its stumpy tower and miniature spire. Down by the mouth of the River Rother a few cottages and small boats constitute Rye Harbour. This is a good birdwatching spot – here among the gravel pits winter wildfowl flock, and paths lead along the shore to Winchelsea.

DON'T MISS

LAMB HOUSE

RYE CASTLE MUSEUM

RYE HARBOUR

THE SEA HAS RECEDED

FROM THE TOWN,

LEAVING IT MAROONED

ON ITS HILL.

Folkestone

Kent

14 miles (23km) east of Ashford

The arrival of the South Eastern Railway in 1842 transformed Folkestone from a minor fishing village into a cross-Channel ferry port and one of the south coast's classier resorts. Within a year the first passenger ship had left for Boulogne, taking four hours over the journey, which meant that the trip from London to Paris could be achieved in a trifling 12 hours. William Cubitt's 19-arch brick railway viaduct, which takes passengers out to the ferries, has been hailed as the most distinguished piece of architecture in the town.

Today, fairground amusements and boats cluster close to the stone pier. A water-powered cliff lift carries visitors up from the foreshore to the West Cliff and the Leas, a spacious promenade with a Mediterranean air, almost a mile long. Handsome terraces and hotels gaze out over the Channel in an area originally planned by Decimus Burton.

Over to the east is the main bathing beach, East Cliff Sands, with a long stretch of open grassland above it and three Martello towers. Walks zig-zag through Folkestone Warren, a tangled wilderness which is now a nature reserve.

Margate

Kent

15 miles (24km) northeast of Canterbury

DON'T MISS

MARGATE CAVES

SHELL GROTTO

DREAMLAND
AMUSEMENT PARK

MARGATE OFFERS
BOTH LOVELY VISTAS
AND TRADITIONAL
SEASIDE FARE.

Margate's reputation as a breezy, boisterous, cheap and cheerful pleasure resort goes back well over 200 years. It was a Margate man, a Quaker glover named Benjamin Beale, who gave the world the bathing machine, which he invented in the 1750s. By 1775 the town marshalled 30 of them, drawn up on its fine, curving beach of golden sand. London trippers used to arrive in seasick droves in sailing boats called Margate hoys, of 80 tons or so. In the 19th century these vessels were replaced by steamers, and the railway reached Margate in the 1840s.

Today, the seafront along Marine Terrace is alive with amusement arcades, bingo parlours, palmists, joke shops and souvenir shops, and places to buy fish and chips, ice cream, candy floss and Margate rock. The colossal amusement park has 25 acres (10ha) of rides with all the fun of the fair. The quieter and older part of the town is close to the harbour, the stone pier and the restored classical Droit House (the 'droits' were the harbour dues). There are pleasant old streets in the older part of Margate and the local history museum is conveniently located in the former town hall. Margate Caves are a popular attraction, and the underground shell grotto on Grotto Hill is a remarkable 18th-century folly whose walls are encrusted with thousands of seashells.

Clacton-on-Sea

Essex

13 miles (21km) southeast of Colchester

CLACTON'S BUSY RESORT DEVELOPED ONLY DURING THE LAST CENTURY.

Essex's answer to Margate, out of sight across the Thames Estuary, is crowded with all the accustomed seaside attractions and pastimes, from old-fashioned donkey rides on the beach, putting greens and boat trips, to up-to-the-minute discos, nightspots and karaoke, with amusement arcades, ballrooms, fairground rides, a roller-skating rink and the Living Ocean aquarium on the pier, a naturist beach and attractive public gardens along the low cliff top above the foreshore. The Princes Theatre and the West Cliff Theatre present star entertainment, there are sightseeing flights from Clacton airstrip and family fun at Magic City – with holograms, a crazy house and an eerie shadow room, as well as a and lounge for the grown-ups.

With all this activity, it is hard to believe that only a hundred years ago there was nothing much here except a couple of Martello towers. Inland, the village of Great Clacton dozed around its medieval church and peaceable inns, the inhabitants occasionally walking the mile (1.5km) to the seashore for a swim. In the 1860s, however, land here went up for sale and a brand-new resort was planned. The prime mover was a railway promoter named Peter Schuyler Bruff, and he was backed by the Woolwich Steam Packet Company, which already ran regular services from London to Harwich and Ipswich and saw prospects of profit.

The virgin town was to have a pier – essential for landing the steamer passengers – a hotel and lodging houses, a promenade along the front with pleasure gardens and villas, a library and a bazaar. The stumpy little pier – later

considerably extended – opened in 1871. At that point in the young resort's life there were two donkeys on the beach, two bathing huts and a few horse-drawn bathing machines, but the Royal Hotel opened in the following year and the new church of St Paul's in 1875. In 1882 the Great Eastern Railway steamed in and, by the time Peter Schuyler Bruff died in 1900, his fledgling had become one of the country's most popular resorts.

Harwich

Essex

16 miles (26km) east of Colchester

DON'T MISS

REDOUBT FORT

PORT OF HARWICH MARITIME MUSEUM

ELECTRIC PALACE CINEMA

HARWICH'S LARGE CONTAINER PORT DOMINATES THE SKYLINE OF THE TOWN.

Harwich is a good place for ship watching as the big ferries ply in and out of Parkeston Quay to the Hook of Holland, Germany and Scandinavia. The town has a long history, which can be followed along its maritime heritage trail. It was planted on the bank of the estuary, where the Stour and the Orwell flow out into the North Sea, by the Earls of Norfolk in the 13th century, and over the next 200 years was used as a base for launching armies against the French. Later the *Mayflower*, the ship that took the Pilgrim Fathers to America in 1620, was often seen in the harbour. She was captained by a Harwich man, Christopher Jones, who lived in King's Head Street. A naval dockyard opened here in the 1660s, and one survivor of this time is the unique treadwheel crane, which was powered by men walking inside its pair of 16ft (5m) wheels. It was still in use when World War I was raging.

Another notable relic is the Electric Palace Cinema of 1911, sadly no longer in regular use, which is the oldest unaltered purpose-built cinema in the country. The High and Low Lighthouses date from 1818, and the church of St Nicholas, built in 1821, has unusual columns and a gallery made of cast-iron.

Aldeburgh
Suffolk
6 miles (10km) southeast of Saxmundham

BOTTOM: FISHING BOATS BEACHED ON THE SHINGLE ARE A COMMON SIGHT AT ALDEBURGH.

BELOW: MOOT HALL, ORIGINALLY BUILT IN THE MARKETPLACE, IS NOW BESIDE THE ENCROACHING SEA.

The River Alde rises near Framlingham and makes its reluctant way eastwards until suddenly, within a hundred yards of the coast, it turns right and, under the disapproving eye of a Martello tower, wanders on to the south for another 10 miles (16km), parallel to the shore. Aldeburgh is immediately to the north of the river's right-hand bend.

A minor seaside resort and fishing village, it is also a major musical centre, known since 1948 for the annual Aldeburgh Festival. (Some events are held in the church, but the main concert hall is in the Maltings at Snape, a few miles inland.) The little half-timbered, flint-and-brick Moot Hall was built in Tudor times as the market hall, presumably in the middle of the marketplace. Now it stands almost on the shingle beach where the fishermen draw up their boats, and half the Tudor town has vanished into the maw of the sea. The building was heavily restored in 1854, when the Jacobean-style chimneys were added.

Today's town extends along the coast down to Slaughden Quay on the Alde. There was ship-building here in the 16th and 17th centuries, and much smuggling in the 18th.

As well as smugglers, this part of the Suffolk coast also attracted writers, including Wilkie Collins, Edward Fitzgerald, the author of the fatalistic

Rubáiyát of Omar Khayyám, and George Crabbe, the poet-clergyman whose grandfather was Customs Collector here and who was born in the town in 1754. It was from him that Benjamin Britten took the story of Peter Grimes. Britten is buried in the church of St Peter and St Paul, as is Elizabeth Garrett Anderson, who was Britain's first woman doctor and a leading campaigner on behalf of women's rights.

Southwold
Suffolk
8 miles (13km) east of Halesworth

BELOW: THE HARBOUR ON THE RIVER BLYTH AT SOUTHWOLD IS HOME TO A RANGE OF SMALL BOATS.

RIGHT: COLOURFUL BATHING HUTS ARE A TRADITIONAL FEATURE OF LIFE AT BRITISH SEASIDE RESORTS.

FAR RIGHT: THE LIGHTHOUSE AT SOUTHWOLD TOWERS OVER THE SMALL HOUSES OF THE TOWN.

The lighthouse and the church tower both rise 100ft (30m) into the sky over Southwold, on its cliff above the North Sea. The gleaming white lighthouse, standing among the houses of the town, dates from the 1880s. The church is some four hundred years older, with splendid examples of Suffolk flushwork – patterns made of flint and stone. It was built here to replace a previous church, which had burned down, and is dedicated to St Edmund, King and Martyr, because Southwold belonged to the rich abbey of Bury St Edmunds. St Edmund was a 9th-century East Anglian king shot to death by the Danes with arrows, like a latter-day St Sebastian, when he refused to renounce his Christian faith. The church has a fine hammerbeam roof, and the painted figures in the panels of the rood- and aisle-screens have been restored. The choir stalls are among the finest in the county. The ancient figure of a man-at-arms, called Southwold Jack, with bloodshot eyes and a stubbly beard, is armed with a sword and a battleaxe with which he strikes a bell to herald services or salute a bride.

The Domesday Book records a substantial tribute of herrings sent to the monks of Bury St Edmunds every year from Southwold, and Buss Creek to the north of the town is named after the 'busses', or herring boats. By the end of the 16th century the town's prosperity was in danger from the same sea from which it earned its living, as the tides threatened to block the harbour mouth with shingle and a cut had to be made through it. In 1659 the town caught fire and most of it was destroyed. It was rebuilt in a style which

has a distinctly Dutch flavour. Six 18-pounder cannon pointing out to sea from Gun Hill were put there in the 18th century, but have never been used. The fishing harbour is to the south, at the mouth of the River Blyth.

BATTLE IN SOLE BAY

In May 1672, during the wars against the Dutch, the allied English and French fleet put into Sole Bay, off Southwold, for fresh water. The commander-in-chief was the future James II, King Charles II's younger brother. During the night the Dutch navy appeared, commanded by the great Admiral De Ruyter, and almost took the allies by surprise. Battle commenced in the morning, and the enemies pounded each other with terrible ferocity all day. James's flagship was so badly battered that he had to shift to another vessel, and in the evening was forced to move yet again. The *Royal James* was set alight by a fireship and blew up, and the English casualties were put at about 2,500 men. Finally the Dutch withdrew, and both sides claimed the victory.

Great Yarmouth
Norfolk
18 miles (29km) east of Norwich

DON'T MISS

ELIZABETHAN HOUSE MUSEUM

MERRIVALE MODEL VILLAGE

TOLHOUSE MUSEUM

ROW III HOUSES

GREAT YARMOUTH IS RENOWNED AS EAST ANGLIA'S MOST POPULAR RESORT.

Like the Alde to the south, the River Yare heads for the sea – through the spreading sandflats and mudflats of Breydon Water – only to be deflected to the south by a narrow spit of land. It was on this peninsula that the port of Yarmouth developed, along the river and with its back turned firmly to the sea.

Here the herring drifters landed their catches and the curing houses smoked the celebrated Yarmouth bloaters. Yarmouth was an active shipbuilding centre, but for centuries its prosperity rested mainly on the vast shoals of herring in the North Sea. Merchants from all over Western Europe and Scandinavia came to the medieval Free Herring Fair, which lasted for 40 days from Michaelmas.

Before World War I more than a thousand fishing boats plied from Yarmouth, but overfishing took its toll and the port turned to servicing North Sea oil and gas operations. There are also regular ferries to the Netherlands.

Running inland from the quayside were the old, cramped alleys called the Rows, so narrow that a special horse-drawn vehicle called a troll cart was developed for moving goods in the town. In 1804 they were numbered, from Row I to Row 145. Yarmouth was badly damaged by bombing during World War II, but parts of the Rows survived, and the Old Merchant's House and Row III Houses are open to the public. Along the river quays are examples of merchants' houses from Tudor to Victorian times.

Cromer

Norfolk

21 miles (34km) north of Norwich

DON'T MISS

CROMER MUSEUM

HENRY BLOGG MUSEUM

ST PETER AND ST PAUL CHURCH

CROMER HAS BEEN A MUCH-FREQUENTED BATHING RESORT SINCE THE 18TH CENTURY.

In 1779 a bathing machine was advertised at Cromer, and soon the rich Norwich banking families of Gurney and Barclay and their Quaker relations began to take holidays here, and to rent or buy houses. The resort developed further in the 19th century. The sandy beach was an attraction, and so (it was said) were the simple manners of the inhabitants, the fact that the sun could be seen both rising and setting in the sea, and the local dressed crab. It was a place for gentlefolk, and there was opposition when the railway arrived in 1877. Hotels and lodging houses now proliferated, the journalist Clement Scott publicised this stretch of coast as 'Poppyland', and a new pier and bandstand were built in the 1900s. The earlier Cromer was a fishing village, which took the place of an earlier one still,

called Shibden, which was consumed by the sea. The impressive church of St Peter and St Paul, whose 160ft (49m) tower is Norfolk's tallest by far, was built in the 14th century. Nearby cottages have been turned into a museum of the area's history and natural history. There is a lifeboat museum, too, and a richly old-fashioned seaside follies show still packs them in at the pier theatre throughout the summertime.

'You should have gone to Cromer, my dear, if you went anywhere. Perry was a week at Cromer once, and he holds it to be the best of all the sea-bathing places. A fine open sea, he says, and very pure air.'

Jane Austen, *Emma (1815)*

Cley next the Sea
Norfolk
4 miles (6km) northwest of Holt

The name 'Cley' is pronounced to rhyme with 'why' and it is not next to the sea any more, and has not been since the reclaiming of marshland for pasture in the 17th century left it a mile (1.5km) or so inland. In earlier days Cley was an important port at the mouth of the River Gleven, ranking second only to King's Lynn on this coast. Wool and, later, cloth was exported to the Netherlands, and the boats brought Dutch tiles back. There is still a small quay on the Gleven, but Cley's most notable feature today is the tremendous 18th-century windmill, with its sturdy brick tower, soaring white sails and conical wooden cap. One of the most photographed windmills in the country, it has been turned into a private house and there has recently been some concern about its preservation.

Among attractive houses of flint and red brick in the village is the unusual Whalebone House, with panels of flint in the walls framed by whalebones. To the south, where the old harbour stood, the church of St Margaret is one of Norfolk's finest, rebuilt on a grand scale in the 14th century and a witness to Cley's prosperity at that time. The Black Death in the 1340s caused the money to run short, and so there is a much smaller chancel than the ample nave might lead you to expect. The two-storey 15th-century porch has fantastic battlements and a fan-vaulted roof, whose bosses are carved with angels and flowers and a woman throwing her distaff at a fox to scare it away from her chickens. The church has numerous fine brasses, including those of John Symonds and his wife in their burial shrouds, with the

ominous words 'Now Thus', and their eight children. The transepts have been in ruins since Tudor days.

Cley is on the part of the north Norfolk coast known to geologists as the North Alluvial Plain, a strip of land along the sea's edge, not more than 2 miles (3km) deep and built up over the last thousand years by sediment brought down by the rivers. Local landowners and farmers helped to create it by building walls and digging ditches to transform the salt-marshes into pastureland. The landscape mingles cattle pasture with salt-marshes, through which creeks wind their way muddily to the sea among banks of shingle and sand. Birds haunt the area in multitudes, and almost the entire coastline is protected by nature reserves.

THE WHALEBONE HOUSE HAS REAL WHALE BONES IN ITS WALLS.

ONE OF CLEY'S MOST PHOTOGRAPHED FEATURES IS ITS 18TH-CENTURY WINDMILL.

THE RIVER GLAVEN FLOWS THROUGH CLEY MARSHES.

Wells-next-the-sea
Norfolk
6 miles (10km) east of Burnham Market

This is a working harbour town with a quayside filled with colourful boats and dock equipment. No longer by the sea, Wells stands on a muddy creek. The embankment is 1 mile (1.5km) long, was built to prevent the harbour from silting up altogether, and provides a pleasant walk to the sea. A delicious local delicacy, pickled samphire, can be bought here.

ABOVE, RIGHT: EVENING LIGHT FALLS ON BOATS IN THE HARBOUR.

RIGHT: A BOAT CREW PREPARE THEIR CATCH OF SHRIMP BY BOILING.

FAR RIGHT: WELLS IS THE ONLY ONE OF THE FORMERLY GREAT PORTS OF EASTERN ENGLAND TO REMAIN COMMERCIALLY VIABLE.

Holkham

Norfolk

2 miles (3km) west of Wells-next-the-sea

Thomas Coke, 1st Earl of Leicester, had the Palladian-style mansion Holkham Hall built between 1734 and 1764. Capability Brown landscaped some of the 3,000 acres of grounds and created the mile-long lake. The hall looks out across the lovely expanse of Holkham Beach. In the 19th century, the sand dunes were planted with Corsican pines, and are now part of Holkham Nature Reserve.

DON'T MISS

HOLKHAM HALL &
BYGONES MUSEUM

HOLKHAM HALL HOUSES A COLLECTION OF GREEK AND ROMAN STATUES.

HOLKHAM DUNES ARE PROTECTED AS PART OF AN IMPORTANT NATURE RESERVE.

Hunstanton

Norfolk

14 miles (23km) north of King's Lynn

HUNSTANTON'S BEACHES ARE BACKED BY STRIKING RED-AND-WHITE-STRIPED CLIFFS.

The only East Anglian seaside resort to face west, Hunstanton has an essentially Victorian atmosphere, with handsome hotels and lovely Esplanade gardens sloping towards the sea. Hunstanton has some remarkable striped cliffs formed by layers of different rocks.

THE LIGHTHOUSE THAT HAS BECOME A SYMBOL OF HUNSTANTON DATES FROM 1830.

Old Hunstanton is steeped in history and legend. It is said that St Edmund was shipwrecked here in AD 855, and was so grateful for being spared a watery death in the Wash that he built a chapel. The 13th-century ruins still stand today, looking out across grey stormy seas from near the old lighthouse. Edmund left Hunstanton soon after and went on to become King of the East Angles. Between AD 869 and 870 Vikings invaded his kingdom and fought bloody battles with him until he was defeated and captured. He refused to renounce his faith and died a particularly unpleasant death.

Edmund's grave was later dug up and his body was found to be uncorrupted. His remains were moved around the country for many years in an attempt to keep them safe from the Vikings. They were eventually kept in Bury St Edmunds, although records are vague about what happened to them later. Some say they were taken to France, others that he was reinterred at Bury after the Reformation.

Members of the Le Strange family have been squires and landlords here for more than 800 years. They laid claim to the beach and, according to one charter, all that is in the sea for as far as a horseman can hurl a spear at low tide. The family still holds the title of Lord High Admiral of the Wash.

Scarborough
North Yorkshire
35 miles (56km) northeast of York

DON'T MISS

SCARBOROUGH CASTLE

ROTUNDA MUSEUM

WOOD END MUSEUM

SEA LIFE & MARINE SANCTUARY

HENRY III GRANTED A CHARTER TO BUILD AN EARLY VERSION OF THE PORT IN 1251.

Scarborough was Britain's first seaside resort, but it had a long history before that. Between the town's twin sandy bays a high cliff juts out into the North Sea. This was the site of a settlement in prehistoric times, and the Romans put a signal station here in the 4th century, part of an early-warning system against sea-raiders. On the site now is the massive medieval castle with its 80ft (24m) keep, outer walls and towers. The fortress withstood many sieges and was shelled from the sea during World War I. George Fox, the founder of the Quakers, was imprisoned here in the

17th century. The town grew up below all this, between the castle cliff and the South Bay harbour. Narrow passageways called The Bolts served as 12th-century public lavatories, automatically flushed twice a day by the sea. When a new quay was built soon after 1300, they survived as alleys. The medieval parish church of St Mary was badly damaged during the Civil War and heavily restored in 1848; the novelist Anne Brontë's grave is in the churchyard.

Scarborough became a spa after a mineral spring was discovered in the 1620s. It was believed such disgusting-tasting water must be good for the human frame, and the local medical men trumpeted the spring as a panacea for ailments, including melancholy and hypochondria. The spa had a smart social life of balls and card parties, and early in the 18th century patients took to swimming in the sea – behaviour previously unheard of. The arrival of the railway from York in 1845 signalled a boom period for the town, and the Victorians have left a splendid legacy of hotels, houses and beautiful terraced gardens. The colossal Grand Hotel, by the Yorkshire architect Cuthbert Brodrick. The 1860s church of St Martin on the Hill, by G F Bodley, is a treasure house of Pre-Raphaelite work, with stained glass by Burne-Jones, Rossetti, William Morris and Ford Madox Brown. In the Rotunda Museum of local history, original display cabinets from 1829 can still be admired. Scarborough Art Gallery is in a Victorian villa of 1845, and the Wood End Museum of natural history is in the former home of the literary Sitwells, and contains many mementos of the family.

Robin Hood's Bay
North Yorkshire
6 miles (10km) southeast of Whitby

The curving expanse of Robin Hood's Bay stretches from North Cheek or Ness Point down to Ravenscar. Near the northern end is the village – often called Bay Town – diving down a steep ravine to the sea, its cottages cramped along narrow alleys and diminutive courtyards, piled so closely on top of one another that they have been compared to sand martins' nests. Constantly menaced by the sea, which eats away at the cliff, the villagers lived for centuries by fishing, combined with the smuggling of brandy, gin, tea and silks brought surreptitiously across from the Netherlands. The writer Leo Walmsley, who lived here from 1894 to 1913, made the most of the smuggling tradition in stories in which the village appears as 'Bramblewick'. In 1885 the railway arrived and brought a new source of income from visitors, and 90 years after that a 40ft (13m) sea wall was built to keep the sea at bay.

Where the connection with Robin Hood comes from is a mystery, but the name apparently goes back at the latest to 1538. According to various local stories, the doughty outlaw took his summer holidays here, or was pursued and escaped by dressing up as one of the fishermen, or perhaps he came here to help the monks of Whitby against the Danes.

Whitby

North Yorkshire

17 miles (27km) northwest of Scarborough

DON'T MISS

WHITBY ABBEY

ST MARY'S CHURCH

WHITBY MUSEUM

WHITBY TOWN IS TERRACED BENEATH THE NORMAN TOWER OF ST MARY'S.

The River Esk makes its way through a deep gorge to reach the sea at Whitby, where the houses of the picturesque former whaling port perch on the steep sides of the cleft. Up on the East Cliff stand the ruins of medieval Whitby Abbey, successor to the one founded here by St Hilda in AD 657 and destroyed by the Danes some 300 years later. Nearby, the parish church of St Mary has a Norman tower and a charming 18th-century interior recalling the inside of a wooden ship – it is the work of the local shipwrights. Observing a coffin being carried up the 199 steps from the town for a funeral inspired Bram Stoker to set part of *Dracula* here. (You can follow a Dracula Trail today and visit the Dracula Experience if you dare!)

The great explorer James Cook learned his seamanship at Whitby, which was a flourishing whaling centre in his time. A statue on the West Cliff commemorates him, and the house he lived in is now a museum. There is material about him in Whitby Museum, too, which also has engaging collections of fossils, bygones and Whitby jet, which was fashionable for mourning jewellery in Victorian Britain.

Marsden Bay
South Tyneside

MARSDEN BAY
WAS FOR YEARS
A FAVOURED HIDING
PLACE FOR SMUGGLERS.

The coast of Durham south of the Tyne was long renowned for its smugglers. The natural caves at the base of the cliffs of Marsden Bay provided hiding places for illicit activity. Most famous of the smugglers was Jack the Blaster, who in 1792 used explosives to increase the size of one of the caves and provide steps from the cliff top. An entrepreneur, he sold refreshments to other smugglers. In the 19th century an underground ballroom was created here, and in the 1930s a lift was installed. It is now a popular pub and eating place called the Marsden Grotto.

The red-and-white striped Souter Lighthouse was erected in 1871 to protect ships from the notorious rocks called Whitburn Steel, just off the coast. It was the first light in the world to be electrically powered. Originally it was nearly a quarter of a mile (400m) from the sea, but erosion has brought the cliff edge much nearer. Now that they are decommissioned and in the care of the National Trust, the lighthouse and its surrounding buildings reward careful exploration. The grassy area north of the light, The Lees, was farmed until the 1930s and then given to the local council as a park. The industrial buildings by the road are the remains of limekilns, used by the local limestone quarries. South of the light, where the Whitburn Coastal Park now lies, was from 1873 to 1968 the site of Whitburn Colliery.

Dunstanburgh Castle
Northumberland
Near Craster, 6 miles (10km) northeast of Alnwick

THE CASTLE LIES A FAIR WALK FROM THE CHARMING FISHING VILLAGE OF CRASTER.

Y ou will have to walk to see Dunstanburgh Castle, because the romantic ruin stands on an outcrop of rock on a lonely stretch of coast, 1 mile (1.5km) from the road. A particularly memorable approach is from the fishing village of Craster, from where it is about twice as far along the coastal path. The site was fortified during the Iron Age, although Thomas, Earl of Lancaster, began the present structure in 1314. Built to protect a small harbour, it was originally surrounded on three sides by the sea (and by a moat on its fourth).

Bamburgh
Northumberland
5 miles (8km) east of Belford

DON'T MISS

BAMBURGH CASTLE

GRACE DARLING MUSEUM

BAMBURGH CASTLE HAS PROVIDED A HISTORICAL BACKDROP TO MANY FILMS.

Northumberland has been called 'the kingdom of castles' because of its number of formidable strongholds. One of the most impressive is Bamburgh Castle, 150ft (46m) up on its almost vertical black crag, from which it glares forbiddingly out to sea across a broad expanse of sand. It seems fitting that it should appear in the Arthurian legends as Joyous Garde, the castle of Sir Lancelot of the Lake, the greatest of the Knights of the Round Table.

The stone keep was built in the 12th century, but much of the castle dates from the period after 1894, when it was renovated by Lord Armstrong, the inventor and armaments magnate. A fine succession of rooms includes a well-stocked armoury, the King's Hall, the keep hall and the kitchens.

In AD 547 an Anglo-Saxon king built a wooden fortress on the rock, and King Oswald of Northumbria, who founded the Lindisfarne monastery in 635, made Bamburgh his capital. It was destroyed by Vikings in the 10th century. The Normans built the present keep. A town grew up under the castle's protection, and in the Middle Ages this boasted a Dominican friary, a market, and fairs in honour of King Oswald and St Aidan. Aidan, of the Lindisfarne monastery, died at Bamburgh in AD 651; the church is dedicated to him.

A museum in the village tells the story of Grace Darling, whose father kept the nearby Longstone Lighthouse. One stormy night in 1838 a steamer struck a rock. Grace and her father twice rowed out in an open boat in huge seas to pick up survivors. The 22-year-old girl's courage caused a sensation and she became a national celebrity.

LEFT TO RIGHT: ST MARY'S ISLAND, BEACHY HEAD; SMEATON'S TOWER, PLYMOUTH; BELOW: NASH POINT, RHOSILLI.

Lighting the Shore

The lighthouse-keepers of the popular stereotype, cooped up for weeks at a time in lonely sea-towers, are figures of the past. Today's lighthouses need no human attendants to operate the lights that are so vital to safety at sea.

Britain's oldest lighthouse is the ruined Roman one on the cliff at Dover. A fire burned in a brazier on top, fanned by the draught up the tower, to aid ships entering Dover harbour. In the Middle Ages beacon lights were maintained here and there along the coast by monks and anchorites. A hermit named Richard Reedbarrow kept a fire burning to warn ships at Spurn Head and on the Dorset coast the Benedictines of Abbotsbury kept a fire burning in St Catherine's Chapel.

Coastal lights and signals were not always evidence of humanitarian principles. According to tradition, the Abbot of Aberbrothock installed a bell on the dangerous Inchcape Reef, offshore from Arbroath on Scotland's east coast, to lure ships to their doom and his profit. When the first lighthouses were proposed for Cornwall, there was determined opposition from the locals, who feared that they would reduce the number of wrecks they were accustomed to plunder.

ABOVE: THE BLACK-
AND-WHITE
LIGHTHOUSE PROTECTS
SHIPS PASSING SPURN
HEAD AT THE MOUTH
OF THE RIVER HUMBER.

In the 1690s a ship-owner named Henry Winstanley built a fantastical-looking lighthouse on the savage Eddystone rocks in the English Channel. He and his lighthouse were swept away by a vengeful storm in 1703. A second, wooden lighthouse burned down in 1735 and was replaced by a simple stone tower, designed by John Smeaton, which became the model for all subsequent tower lighthouses.

In England and Wales the Brotherhood of Trinity House, founded by Henry VIII, was responsible for building lighthouses. In Scotland this duty fell to the Commissioners of Northern Lights, and a period of intense activity around the turn of the 18th and 19th centuries was dominated by the remarkable Stevenson dynasty. The great Robert Stevenson planted the Bell Rock lighthouse on the Inchcape Reef. His son Alan built the 200-ft (60m) tower on the Muckle Flugga Rock in Shetland, still the northernmost lighthouse in Britain.

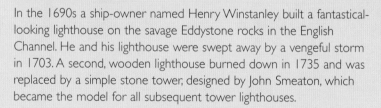

ABOVE: MUMBLES
HEAD LIGHTHOUSE IN
WALES PROTECTS SHIPS
FROM A PAIR OF ROCKY
ISLETS.

RIGHT: LONGSTONE
LIGHTHOUSE IN THE
FARNE ISLANDS.

Farne Islands
Northumberland
Between 2 and 5 miles (3–8km) off the coast at Bamburgh

The National Trust acquired the Farne Islands in 1925, and protects them as a bird sanctuary. Farne is Celtic for land, and these 30 or so bits of sea-lapped dolerite rock with their stacks and cliffs can be reached by boat from Seahouses when it is not too rough. Inner Farne and Staple Island are open at limited times to visitors, who are strongly recommended to wear hats!

St Aidan used to come to the islands from Lindisfarne for lonely prayer and meditation, and St Cuthbert, the Northumbrian shepherd boy who became the north of England's most admired saint, lived as a hermit for a time on Inner Farne. He built himself a hut, and there are stories of him reproving the greedy, thoughtless birds for not behaving in a more Christian manner. He died on the island in AD 687. A chapel there survives, built in his memory in the 14th century. Friendly grey seals breed on the islands and puffins make tunnels in the sand or take over rabbit burrows. They are called Tommy Noddies locally, because of the way their heads bob as they walk along. Other nesting birds include petrel, guillemot, cormorant, all sorts of tern and the eider ducks, known as St Cuthbert's chicks or cuddy ducks because the saint particularly loved them.

THE MAIN ATTRACTION OF THE FARNE ISLANDS IS THE WILDLIFE, ESPECIALLY SEABIRDS.

BOAT TRIPS USUALLY PASS CLOSE ENOUGH TO SEE THE NESTING SITES OF THE BIRDS.

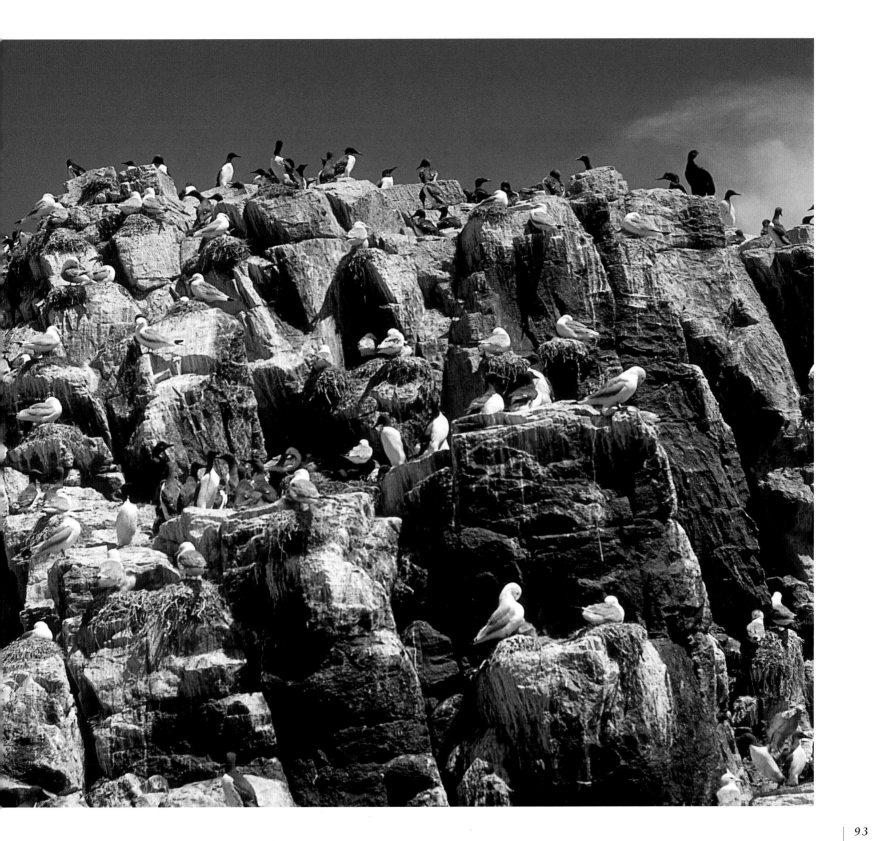

THE PENITENT RAVEN

'One day some ravens which had long inhabited the island were seen tearing the straw from the roof of the visitors' house and carrying it off to build their nests. The saint reproved them with a slight gesture of his right hand and told them to leave the monks' property alone. They merely scorned his command. "In the Name of Jesus Christ, depart forthwith!" he shouted. "Do not dare remain to do more damage."

They flew off shamefacedly almost before he had finished speaking. Three days later one of a pair of them returned and, finding Cuthbert digging, stood before him, with feathers outspread and head bowed low to its feet in sign of grief.

BOATS CAN TAKE VISITORS
TO STAPLE ISLAND IN THE
BIRD BREEDING SEASON
(MAY TO JULY).

Using whatever signs it could to express contrition it very humbly asked pardon. When Cuthbert realised what it meant, he gave permission for them all to return. Back they came with a fitting gift – a lump of pig's lard.'

Venerable Bede, *Life of Cuthbert* (8th century)

(trans J F Webb, Penguin Classics)

Lindisfarne Castle

Northumberland

13 miles (21km) southeast of Berwick-upon-Tweed

Joined at low tide by a causeway to the mainland, Holy Island (known as Lindisfarne before 1082) retains the sense of isolation that drew monks and hermits here from the Dark Ages onwards. The most famous monk was St Cuthbert (died AD 687), bishop of the monastery. The museum beside the ruins of 12th-century Lindisfarne recounts the life of the early monks.

A STATUE OF A MONK AT HOLY ISLAND COMMEMORATES ST AIDAN'S WORK.

Lindisfarne Castle was built in the 1540s and restored in 1903 by the architect Sir Edwin Lutyens; its interior is a combination of the 16th century, comfortable Edwardian furnishings and Lutyens's quirks and foibles. If planning to visit the castle, take note of the signs for safe crossing times.

THE HOLY ISLAND SANDS MUDFLATS ARE PART OF LINDISFARNE NATIONAL NATURE RESERVE.

THE ROMANTIC CASTLE
OF LINDISFARNE
IS ACCESSIBLE
ONLY AT LOW TIDE.

Lower Largo
Fife
2 miles (3km) northeast of Leven

CALM, TRANQUIL LOWER LARGO WAS ONCE A THRIVING FISHING PORT. FIFE'S COASTLINE IS A GREAT DRAW FOR VISITORS THROUGHOUT THE YEAR.

The inspiration for one of fiction's most famous characters was born at here in 1676. In 1695, Alexander Selkirk, a shoemaker's son, was summoned to answer for 'indecent behaviour' in church, but had already run away to sea. Serving on expeditions in the Pacific, in 1704 he was marooned on Juan Fernandez Island after a quarrel with his captain. He survived alone for four years until an English ship rescued him. His adventures inspired Daniel Defoe's *Robinson Crusoe*. A statue of him in his goatskins adorns the cottage in which he was born.

Lower Largo was once a fishing port on Largo Bay, but the last fishing boat was sold in the 1940s and the village is now a retirement colony and holiday resort, with a sandy beach and golf links.

Upper Largo, inland, has the church where Alexander Selkirk's parents are buried. Sir Andrew Wood, who led two Scottish ships to a notable triumph over five English vessels off Dunbar in 1498, is also buried there. He had a canal built from his house to the church and liked to be rowed to services in his eight-oared barge.

Peterhead
Aberdeenshire
27 miles (44km) north of Aberdeen

DON'T MISS

ARBUTHNOT MUSEUM
& ART GALLERY

PETERHEAD IS PART OF
THE BUSY FISHING
INDUSTRY ALONG THE
SCOTTISH COASTLINE.

Peterhead is Scotland's most easterly town, and owed its early development to the Earls Marischal. The Arbuthnot Museum illuminates the history of the town, which in the 18th century became for a time a smart spa. The harbour proved a more durable asset, however; in the 1880s a prison was built on the bay and the felons were put to work on harbour improvements. In the 19th century Peterhead became a leading whaling port, later turning to herring fishing, then whitefish.

In 1990 Peterhead was the premier whitefish port in Europe, with £70 million worth of catches landed in the harbour. However, overfishing and the European Community's quotas have made the future uncertain.

It was at Peterhead late in December 1715 that the Old Pretender (King James III of England and VIII of Scotland), landed for the one and only time on Scottish soil. His standard had been raised at Braemar in September and a small army of Highlanders rallied to it, to fight an inconclusive engagement at Sheriffmuir in November. James soon decided that the cause was hopeless and returned to France. The young George Keith, 5th Earl Marischal, and his younger brother James, who had joined the rising, had to flee to mainland Europe, too, later to distinguish themselves in the service of Frederick the Great.

Bonar Bridge
Highland
14 miles (23km) west of Dornoch

Rising far away in the mountainous interior of the old county of Sutherland, the River Oykell heads southeast through the Kyle of Sutherland loch to the Dornoch Firth. Where the loch narrows towards the firth, the village of Bonar Bridge arose. The bridge was built by Thomas Telford to replace the old ferry after a disaster in 1809, which killed over 100 people. Dornoch Firth resembles an inland loch at this western end, but widens out into a broad estuary nearer the North Sea, with sandy beaches on either shore.

The small resort town of Dornoch was Sutherland's county town, and the bishops of Caithness had their cathedral here. It is said that 16 earls of Sutherland lie buried in the church. Inland from Bonar Bridge lies country where the notorious Highland Clearances of the 18th

century are still remembered. Landowners removed crofters from the inland valleys to make room for sheep. A road goes to Ardgay and westwards through Strath Carron to the church at Croick, where the bewildered local people scratched despairing messages on the glass of the window.

Janet Horne, the last person to be executed for witchcraft in Scotland, was burned at Dornoch in 1727. The Witch's Stone in Littletown commemorates her (although the date on the stone is erroneously given as 1722).

Gairloch

Highland

7 miles (11km) northwest of Kinlochewe

THE COVE AT GAIRLOCH PRESENTS CLEAR BLUE WATERS AND SANDY BEACHES.

THE OUTER HEBRIDES CAN BE SEEN OVER THE WATER FROM GAIRLOCH.

As late as 1960 Gairloch still made its living from the sea, as the Minch fishing boats landed their catches at the pier. Today it is a holiday resort and a centre for touring the wild and dramatic mountains of Wester Ross. Beside the loch of the same name, the village has a sandy beach and there are sailing and sea-angling trips to be enjoyed, as well as the Heritage Museum. Loch Gairloch is geologically interesting because it displays the two principal rock types of the northwestern coastline. The northern shore is made of reddish Torridonian sandstone, but the southern shoreline is grey Lewisian gneiss. There are sandy beaches along the northern shore and a coast road leads up to Melvaig, with sea views to Skye and the Outer Hebrides. The A832 leads northeast from Gairloch to Poolewe, for boat trips on Loch Ewe and the fabulous Inverewe Gardens. To the south is the beautiful 12-mile (19km) stretch of Loch Maree.

Shieldaig

Highland

9 miles (15km) north of Kishorn

Vying with Plockton as one of the most attractive villages in the Highlands, Shieldaig, with its white-harled and slate-roofed cottages, lies close to the head of Loch Shieldaig in some of Scotland's most breathtaking scenery. Loch Shieldaig was always known for its herrings, though no longer, and indeed the name was originally Sildvik, which is Norse for herring bay. The loch opens into Loch Torridon, by common consent one of the most magical of all Scotland's beautiful lochs. To the south lie the mountains, moors and deer forest of the Applecross Peninsula, and a coast road, opened in 1976 to link the scattered crofting settlements together, commanding views over the Inner Sound to Raasay and Skye. Going the other way, east from Shieldaig, the A896 road along Upper Loch Torridon yields awesome prospects of the red sandstone crags of Beinn Alligin and Liathach, rising above 3,000ft (915m). The National Trust for Scotland owns the superb 16,000-acre (6,500ha) Torridon Forest Estate, which formerly belonged to the Earls of Lovelace, with its rare eagles and wildcats, mountain goats and deer. There is a good visitor centre and a deer museum.

LEFT TO RIGHT:
GANNETS, BASS ROCK;
PUFFIN, SCOTLAND;
BIRDWATCHING AT
BASS ROCK, NEAR
NORTH BERWICK.

coastal birdwatching

Both for scenic beauty and for wildlife interest, the British coastline is outstanding.

It has everything from towering cliffs to shallow estuaries, shingle beaches and sand dunes. The variety and richness in both habitat and wildlife is often stunning and, whatever the season, there is always something to see. Many of Britain's best sites for birdwatching are on the coast, including the Farne Islands, and the RSPB reserves at Minsmere on the Suffolk coast, Titchwell in Norfolk, and Leighton Moss in Lancashire. From April until July, the cliffs of Britain are home to vast numbers of breeding seabirds, particularly to the north and west – a notable exception is Bempton Cliffs on the east coast, famous for its nesting gannets. Watch a seabird colony for even a short time and it soon becomes apparent that each species has its own special nesting requirements. Razorbills prefer crevices and boulders close to the sea; shags and fulmars nest on broad ledges; while kittiwakes and guillemots are often densely packed on narrow ledges overhanging sheer drops. Puffins dig burrows into the grassy slopes higher up the cliffs, while herring gulls and lesser black-backed gulls are found in loose colonies among the tussocks of vegetation.

Estuaries and mudflats found all around the coast provide superb opportunities for birdwatching throughout the year. The estuaries are important staging posts for migrants, and from autumn to spring vast numbers of migrant birds may be seen enjoying these rich feeding grounds. One of the most conspicuous birds of the coast is the redshank. Often called 'the sentinels of the marsh', these red-legged waders are alert and quick to utter their alarm call. This brings potential danger to the attention of other wading birds such as

ABOVE: BIRDWATCHING
ON THE OUSE
WASHES, FROM A
WILDLIFE AND
WETLAND TRUST
OBSERVATORY.

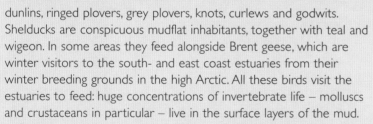

dunlins, ringed plovers, grey plovers, knots, curlews and godwits. Shelducks are conspicuous mudflat inhabitants, together with teal and wigeon. In some areas they feed alongside Brent geese, which are winter visitors to the south- and east coast estuaries from their winter breeding grounds in the high Arctic. All these birds visit the estuaries to feed: huge concentrations of invertebrate life – molluscs and crustaceans in particular – live in the surface layers of the mud.

Beaches and sand dunes, especially in southern Britain, suffer more than most habitats from human disturbance. Nesting birds also suffer, and it is only in certain protected areas in England that terns, oystercatchers, ringed plovers and black-headed gulls can rest in peace. Further north in Britain the beaches are less disturbed and you are more likely to encounter nesting birds. Always be on the lookout for signs of alarmed or distressed birds in these areas during the breeding season.

ABOVE: FEEDING TIME
FOR THE GANNETS.
LEFT PREVIOUS PAGE:
SEABIRDS ON ROCKS
OFF BALCARY BAY,
SCOTLAND.

RIGHT: THE BIRD
COLONY AT INNER
FARNE, OWNED BY THE
NATIONAL TRUST.

Isle of Skye
Highland

DON'T MISS

ARMADALE CASTLE GARDENS
& MUSEUM OF THE ISLES

DUNVEGAN CASTLE

THE CUILLIN HILLS ARE ONE OF THE MOST BEAUTIFUL BRITISH MOUNTAIN RANGES.

Skye's name is Norse, meaning 'isle of clouds', and the southwestern part of the island has some of the heaviest rainfall on the whole of the British coast. All the same, there is a powerful magic about Skye and the visitor attractions can become uncomfortably crowded in summer.

Skye is the largest island of the Inner Hebrides, covering some 535 square miles (1386 sq km). It is a peculiar shape, rather like a giant lobster with the claws to the northwest, and lochs bite deep into it, creating numerous peninsulas. The southwestern one, Sleat, is known as 'the garden of Skye' for the luxuriance of its vegetation. To the northwest, the black, jagged peaks of the Cuillins (pronounced 'Coolins') rise to 3,309ft (1,009m). Boats from Elgol penetrate to the heart of them through Lock Coruisk. Northwest again is Dunvegan Castle, stronghold of the MacLeod chiefs since the 13th century. On the Trotternish Peninsula is the Quiraing, one of the country's strangest rock formations.

ABOVE, RIGHT: SKYE'S MYSTICAL NATURE IS A MAJOR DRAW FOR VISITORS.

DUNVEGAN LOCH CAN BE REACHED BY BOAT FROM THE CASTLE GROUNDS

Plockton
Highland
5 miles (8km) northeast of Kyle of Lochalsh

BELOW: DOMINION OF PALM AND PINE: A VIEW OVER PLOCKTON TO LOCH CARRON.

RIGHT: THE GULF STREAM ENCOURAGES MEDITERRANEAN PLANTS IN PLOCKTON.

Palm trees grow in Plockton, encouraged by the mild Gulf Stream air. Also encouraged are small-boat sailors, holidaymakers and retired people, who come to this beautiful haven on Loch Carron, with its tidy cottages commanding marvellous views seawards, or inland to the mountains and forests. At one time the harbour, protected by a promontory running out into the loch like a natural pier, was busy with cargo schooners plying to and from Baltic ports, and with the local fishing boats. Herring was

taken by sea down to Glasgow, Greenock and the Clyde, and salt and other necessities were brought back. All that changed with the railway's arrival at Kyle of Lochalsh in 1898 and the concentration of traffic there.

Along the southern shore of Loch Carron and extending far inland is the National Trust for Scotland's magnificent Balmacara Estate, covering thousands of acres of woodland, glittering streams and quiet reflective lochs. To the east along the loch shore, Strome Ferry was another thriving port in its time. It faces across the narrow neck of the inner loch to the ruins of Strome Castle, once a formidable stronghold of the MacDonalds. It fell to a siege by the Mackenzies in 1602, allegedly because the castle's womenfolk carelessly emptied water into the gunpowder magazine, so leaving the stronghold defenceless.

KEEPING SUNDAY SPECIAL
The west of Scotland has a strong tradition of observing the Sabbath day, and there were riots in Strome Ferry in the summer of 1873, when two steamers with cargoes of fish arrived at the pier in the very early hours of a Sunday morning. Unloading the cargo began, but a crowd of 50 locals gathered, stormed the pier and stopped the work. A handful of police arrived the next day, but was not equal to the situation. Over the next few days the police strength built up to 160 men and it was only with the intervention of the local Free Church ministers that a potentially violent situation was defused.

Inveraray
Argyll & Bute
19 miles (31km) northeast of Lochgilphead

THE BELL TOWER NEAR THE HOTEL ON THE BANKS OF LOCH FYNE WAS BUILT IN 1920.

INVERARY'S HILLS OFFER SOME OF THE MOST BEAUTIFUL VISTAS IN SCOTLAND.

Clan Campbell's capital stands on the west bank of Loch Fyne, deep among the mountain fastnesses of Argyll. The original settlement of heather-thatched cottages huddled in the protective shadow of the castle, the stronghold of the Campbell chiefs, who became Dukes of Argyll. In 1743 the 3rd Duke resolved to build a brand-new castle and a brand-new town, rather further away, and these were built over the next 70 years and more. The principal planners and architects were Roger Morris, William Adam (father of the more famous Robert) and Robert Mylne. Inveraray Castle itself is a turreted mock-Gothic pile.

Its superb interiors by Mylne were restored after a severe fire in 1975.

In the town, the inn and the jail (now open as a tourist attraction) were among the first of the new buildings, along with the pier for the fishing boats. The town's kindly motto was 'May you always have a catch of herring', but the Loch Fyne fishery is a thing of the past. The town's dignified main street runs from the old market cross past Mylne's parish church, which was divided in two by a wall inside, to separate the services conducted in Gaelic from those in English.

Brodick
North Ayrshire
The Isle of Arran

The setting of Brodick in its wide bay, backed by high peaks with Brodick Castle rising from the trees on the lower slopes, is remarkably beautiful. The castle, formerly owned by the Dukes of Hamilton, was taken over by the National Trust for Scotland in 1957. Retaining the warm and surprisingly intimate air of a family home, its garden is one of the most charming on the west coast, with semi-tropical plants and trees and a delightful water garden.

The original village of Brodick was on the north side of the bay, below the castle, and the remains of this earlier settlement can be seen at Cladach.

THE GLENS AROUND BRODICK ARE POPULAR WITH WALKERS AND PICNICKERS.

BRODICK ENJOYS AN IMPRESSIVE SETTING; GOAT FELL TOWERS IN THE DISTANCE.

Culzean Castle

South Ayrshire

4 miles (6km) west of Maybole

CULZEAN CASTLE BLENDS A CASTELLATED FACADE WITH ITALIANATE INTERIORS. THERE ARE LOFTY VIEWS ACROSS THE SEA FROM THE SPLENDID CIRCULAR SALOON.

Culzean (pronounced 'Cullane') is the National Trust for Scotland's most popular property. It has 563 lush green acres (228ha) of wild gardens and leafy woodland riddled with trails. You can discover a walled garden, an aviary, a deer park and lots of follies dotted around.

The golden stone castle, romantically set right at the edge of the cliffs, is handsome rather than beautiful, with its baronial towers and castellated roofline. It is reached via a bridge, and rises high above a terraced garden. Inside, it is an 18th-century showhome, the masterpiece of Scottish architect Robert Adam, who worked on it from 1777 to 1792 for the powerful Kennedy family, who had dominated this part of Ayrshire since the 12th century.

Highlights include the graceful oval staircase and the Circular Saloon. The top floor was granted to General Eisenhower in 1945, for his lifetime, as a thanks from the people of Scotland for American help during World War II.

Portpatrick
Dumfries & Galloway
6 miles (10km) south of Stranraer

THE LIGHTHOUSE IS A VANTAGE POINT FOR THE ROCKY HARBOUR OF PORTPATRICK.

What Gretna Green was to runaway English couples, so was Portpatrick to eloping lovers from Ireland – a place where they could be married with no inconvenient questions asked. Until 1826 the Church of Scotland ran a profitable trade in quick and easy weddings here: 'landed on Saturday, called on Sunday, married on Monday', as the saying went. The Rhinns Peninsula at Scotland's southwest corner is the closest point to Ireland, and Portpatrick was the Scottish end of the 21-mile (33.5-km) passage to Donaghadee in Ulster. The mails to Ireland took this route, while Irish cattle in bellowing thousands came the other way.

The snag was that Portpatrick's harbour lay at the mercy of the savage southwesterly gales. A pier was built in the 1770s, but it was not adequate and new harbour works on a massive scale began in 1820. The sea swept them all away, and in 1849 the packet boats carrying mail, cargo and passengers to Ireland were transferred to nearby Stranraer. Portpatrick was left to develop as a pleasant small resort for sailing, sea fishing, and nowadays water sports. The 17th-century church has an unusual Irish-style round tower, and the graveyard is the final resting place of many who died in shipwrecks on this harsh coast.

Morecambe

Lancashire

3 miles (5km) northwest of Lancaster

THE FURNESS PENINSULA SHELTERS THE VAST EXPANSE OF MORECAMBE BAY.

Morecambe is famous for its seaside promenade, which is 4 miles (6.5km) long and provides every holiday amusement you could imagine, from theatres, funfairs and amusement arcades to a modern leisure park and entertainment complex. The town's seafront renaissance has included award-winning public projects such as the Platform Arts Centre and the Stone Jetty, a breathtaking place to sit and watch the famous Morecambe Bay sunset. There is a new statue of the town's favourite son, too –

Eric Morecambe, who took his stage name from his boyhood home and became as popular as the resort.

All this is a long way from Morecambe's humble origins as the little fishing village of Poulton-le-Sands, though the boats still fish locally for whitebait, cockles and shrimps. The sands are vast and flat and, although it is possible to walk across the bay to Grange, treacherous currents, quicksands and the speed of the incoming tide make this extremely dangerous without an official guide.

Blackpool

Lancashire

15 miles (24km) west of Preston

The North's champion brash, cheerful, noisy pleasure-ground has been drawing visitors in droves for a hundred years and more. In 1900 the count was 3 million people a year. By the 1960s, when 150,000 holidaymakers arrived expectantly in Blackpool every average summer day, the annual figure peaked at 8 million.

Blackpool is still packing them in. It made its reputation as the top resort for the millhands of the booming Lancashire textile industry before World War I, but it has always kept up with the times. Its miles of inviting sands still offer safe swimming and the traditional donkey rides and Punch and Judy shows, but in case of disappointing weather an enormous indoor beach called the Sandcastle provides 300ft (90m) water chutes and wave pools. The massed amusement arcades of Britain's slot machine capital come equipped with video technology, and the Pleasure Beach funfair boasts the latest spine-chilling rides and roller-coasters. In 1990 the biggest ferris wheel in Europe, 180ft (55m) high, opened on the central pier. The celebrated Illuminations, which clothe the front with gigantic daisy chains of glittering light on autumn nights, now have the benefits of lasers, fibre optics and computer control.

Blackpool has everything. It has three piers and a 7-mile (11km) promenade. It has theatres, dancing, discos and nightspots. It has ice- and roller-skating rinks and waxworks. For quieter moments there is good shopping, an enjoyable collection in the Grundy Art Gallery, and the formal Italian gardens, model village and boating lake in Stanley Park.

BLACKPOOL'S ROLLER-COASTER RIDE IS ONE OF THE RESORT'S TOP DRAWS FOR VISITORS.

THE FAMOUS TOWER HAS BEEN A LANDMARK IN LANCASHIRE SINCE 1894.

Blackpool Tower once had a zoo, a circus and the world's longest bar. Opened in the teeth of local opposition, the Tower was pre-fabricated in Manchester and brought to Blackpool by train to be assembled. Half the height of the Eiffel Tower in Paris, on which it was modelled, it stands 518ft 9in (158m) tall, with remarkable views from the top.

Llandudno

Conwy

3 miles (5km) north of Conwy

Llandudno is delightfully situated between the two looming limestone headlands of the Great Orme and the Little Orme and has a wide, sweeping sandy beach. It was developed in the 1850s by the local landowners, the Mostyn family, and beautifully planned, with a 2-mile (3km) promenade along the sweetly curving North Shore and a grid of wide, tree-lined streets. The town has retained its Victorian character, dignity and charm, and has the best shopping in North Wales.

The handsome Victorian pier extends 2,296ft (700m) out into the bay, and the town has all the expected seaside entertainments: boat trips, band concerts, theatre shows, discos, dancing, cabaret, sailing and fishing, riding and pony-trekking. Llandudno is an entirely appropriate home for the Alice in Wonderland Centre, in the Rabbit Hole, with its displays on this quintessential Victorian fantasy. The original Alice was the daughter of the Liddell family of Oxford, who brought her here for summer holidays as a child. Their house was where the Gogarth Abbey Hotel stands now, on the West Shore. A large collection of dolls is at Childhood Revisited, with toys, lace and fans, a model railway and a collection of motorcycles. Llandudno Museum covers the local history, and Oriel Mostyn is a lively art gallery.

LLANDUDNO STILL RETAINS ITS VICTORIAN ELEGANCE AND TIMELESS CHARM.

Copper was mined on the Great Orme in the Bronze Age and the mine has recently been opened to the public. In the 6th century, St Tudno established his mission here. The town is named after him, as the *llan* or 'holy enclosure' of Tudno, and the little medieval church on the headland is dedicated to him. On the lower slopes of the Great Orme are semi-tropical gardens, and higher up is a country park. There are several ways to the 679ft (207m) summit. One is the mile-long (1.5km) cable-car ride, which is Britain's longest. Another is the electric tramway, which began operating in 1902 and until 1958 was powered by steam. A third is by road from the scenic Marine Drive, opened in 1878, which winds its way around the headland. Up at the top are a new interpretative centre and a nature trail, and from here there are wonderful views inland to the Snowdonian peaks and seawards to the Isle of Man.

LLANDUDNO AND THE WHITE RABBIT

At the age of 80 Alice Liddell, the real-life heroine of *Alice in Wonderland* and *Through the Looking-Glass*, remembered the author Lewis Carroll's visits to Llandudno during summer holidays when she was young, 'and our games on the sandhills together'. She was the daughter of Henry Liddell, Dean of Christ Church, Oxford, and a colleague of Carroll, who was a family friend and adored the young Alice. So perhaps it was the rabbits on the Great Orme that inspired the immortal figure of the White Rabbit and Alice's adventures in the mysterious rabbit hole.

LEFT, TOP: THE TOWN'S PIER, BADLY DAMAGED BY FIRE IN 1994, HAS BEEN FULLY RESTORED.

LEFT: THE ROCKY SHORE OF THE GREAT ORME, WHERE COPPER WAS ONCE MINED.

Conwy
Conwy
3 miles (5km) south of Llandudno

THE IMPRESSIVE
CONWY CASTLE
WAS BUILT BETWEEN
1283 AND 1289.

The eight huge, round, impressive drum towers of Edward I's superb 13th-century castle dominate this pleasant little town at the mouth of the River Conwy. The massive castle walls are 15ft (4.5m) thick and matched by the virtually complete town walls with gates and their barbican still intact.

Three bridges span the river beside the castle – a modern road bridge, Stephenson's tubular railway bridge of 1848 and Thomas Telford's suspension bridge of 1826, which has 'medieval' towers to match those of the castle. This bridge is now in the care of the National Trust.

Another National Trust property in Conwy is the fascinating 14th-century Aberconwy House, the only medieval merchant's house to survive in this once-thriving seaport. It now contains a heritage centre telling the story of the town. Visitors, though only a few at a time, can also see Britain's smallest house (verified by the *Guinness Book of Records*), which is just 6ft (2m) wide by 10ft (3m) high.

TELFORD'S BRIDGE IS
USED AS A FOOTPATH;
THE NEW ROAD BRIDGE
OPENED IN 1958.

119

Menai Bridge
Isle of Anglesey
2 miles (3km) east of Llanfair P G

As its name suggests, this little Anglesey town owes its existence principally to the suspension bridge, which the great engineer Thomas Telford designed to carry his London to Holyhead road over the powerful tides and swirling currents of the Menai Strait. The bridge opened to traffic in 1826, replacing the previous ferry, though it swung so violently in high winds that coachmen and passengers were sometimes too frightened to cross it. With a central span of 579ft (177m), this was the largest suspension bridge in the world when it was completed, and one of the supreme engineering feats of the 19th century. There is a fine view of the bridge from the promenade called Belgian Walk, which was built during World War I by refugees from Belgium. A causeway leads out into the strait to Church Island and the simple 15th-century church dedicated to St Tysilio, a wandering Christian missionary who built a humble church on this spot in the 7th century.

The town also boasts an art gallery and a butterfly farm. A little to the west, the A5 road and the railway cross the strait on another bridge, originally designed by Robert Stephenson in 1850, and replaced after a serious fire in 1970.

THE MENAI BRIDGE IS REGARDED BY MANY AS ONE OF THOMAS TELFORD'S FINEST ACHIEVEMENTS.

Llanddwyn Island

Isle of Anglesey

3 miles (5km) southwest of Newborough

THE CROSS AT LLANDWYN IS A MONUMENT TO THE LOCAL SAINT, DWYN.

THE ISLAND IS IN FACT A PENINSULA, LINKED TO THE MAINLAND AT ALL BUT VERY HIGH TIDES.

Off the southwest coast of Anglesey, Llanddwyn Island is named after St Dwyn, or Dwynwen, a misty figure from far back in the Dark Ages of the 5th and 6th centuries. She was one of the many children of the legendary King Brychan, whose offspring numbered anything from 12 to 63, according to varying traditions. Dwyn was a devout Christian and determined to preserve her virginity, so when a suitor named Maelon wanted to marry her, she sadly rejected him and became a nun. At the same time she earnestly prayed to God that all true lovers should either achieve their desires or be freed of love's fever. She became the unofficial patron saint of lovers in Wales and her church at Llanddwyn attracted numerous pilgrims. Many came to consult the fishes in the saint's holy well, whose movements foretold the future. Today's visitors come for the vast expanse of sand and dunes, with breathtaking views of the Snowdonian mountains across the water. The island is part of the Warren Nature Reserve.

Portmeirion

Gwynedd

2 miles (3km) southwest of Penrhyndeudraeth

Portmeirion is unique. It is a village with no inhabitants. It is completely artificial, has no history and is the inspired creation of one man. It is also one of the most magical places on earth, a vision of towers and domes, courtyards and arches, multi-coloured houses, statues and fountains, stairways and shops, grottos and cool colonnades. Peacocks promenade everywhere you look and at every turning there are fresh, intriguing perspectives.

Portmeirion's creator, Clough Williams-Ellis, cut his teeth as an architect in the Garden City movement. In 1925 he bought a 19th-century house and a tangled, overgrown area of land on the north bank of the sandy estuary of the Glaslyn and the Dwyryd, which had been owned for years by an eccentric recluse. He set about bringing to life a fantasy Mediterranean village on the cliffside, which occupied him for more than 50 years.

Portmeirion was the setting for the 1960s TV classic *The Prisoner* and its devotees still make pilgrimages here. The village stands in a large woodland, and there is even a cemetery for the estate's dogs. It is a touching place, and the tradition of burying much-loved pets there has been continued to the present day.

THE CONVINCING BOAT THAT IS MOORED HERE IS ACTUALLY MADE OF CONCRETE. PORTMEIRION HAS BREATHTAKING VIEWS OF THE BEAUTIFUL GLASLYN ESTUARY.

Aberystwyth
Ceredigion
34 miles (55km) northeast of Cardigan

Aberystwyth has taken a leading part in modern Welsh patriotism. This pleasant seaside town has a good claim to be the Oxbridge of Wales. The Welsh Language Society has its base here, Wales's first university opened here in the 1870s and the town is home to the National Library of Wales, whose unrivalled collection of books and material relating to Wales and the Celtic countries contains venerable manuscripts of early Welsh poetry and laws.

Aberystwyth's promenade runs along the gracefully curving shore, backed by Victorian terraces. The ruins of a 13th-century castle built by Edward I stand on the headland to the south, with the yacht harbour beyond. Britain's longest electric cliff railway, opened in 1896, runs very slowly and gently up a 2-in-1 gradient to the 430-foot (131m) high summit of Constitution Hill. At the top there is a Camera Obscura, whose all-seeing eye gazes hawk-like over 1,000 square miles (2,590 sq km) of spectacular scenery.

ABERYSTWYTH HAS A SMALL HARBOUR AND A BEACH OF SHINGLE AND SAND.

THE BEACH AT THE LARGEST RESORT ON CARDIGAN BAY IS RARELY CROWDED.

Fishguard

Pembrokeshire

9 miles (14km) northeast of St David's

In the 1971 film of *Under Milk Wood*, the picturesque oldest part of Fishguard – the Lower Town down by the harbour – did duty for Dylan Thomas's fictional seaport of Llareggub. It has appeared in other films, too, including *Moby Dick*. The photogenic town's real, Welsh, name is Abergwaun and it stands where the River Gwaun flows out to sea.

A fishing harbour and coastal port in its time, Fishguard was a centre for trade with Ireland and Chester, and late in the 18th century some 50 coastal cargo boats plied from here, exporting oats and salted herring. Today the beautiful harbour shelters small sailing craft and the yachting fraternity. The Royal Oak Inn has mementos of the last invasion of Britain, a comical episode when a small army of Frenchmen landed here in 1797, and St Mary's Church has the grave of the redoubtable local heroine Jemima Nicholas. A woman of formidable physique and alarming aspect, she led the local resistance, capturing no fewer than 14 of the enemy single-handed, wielding only a pitchfork. You can buy traditional Welsh laver bread (made from seaweed) in Fishguard, or you can catch the ferry for the short crossing to Rosslare in Ireland from the harbour at Goodwick, where a 2,000ft (610m) breakwater was constructed before World War I to create a deep-water harbour.

HISTORIC HIGHLIGHT

One of the greatest days in Fishguard's history came on 22 February 1797, during the Napoleonic Wars, when three enemy ships landed a rabble of some 1,400 French soldiers and ex-convicts near Carreg Wastad Point, under an American commander.

The soldiers were meant to march on Chester and Liverpool, but in fact took the opportunity to get thoroughly drunk. The local people reacted vigorously and – so the story has it – the bemused invaders mistook the traditional red cloaks of the Welsh womenfolk for the traditional scarlet uniforms of the British infantry. They surrendered on 24 February and articles of peace were subsequently signed in the Royal Oak Inn.

LOW TIDE PROVIDES THE OPPORTUNITY FOR SOME ESSENTIAL RUNNING REPAIRS.

THE LOWER TOWN AT THE HARBOUR IS FISHGUARD'S MOST PICTURESQUE PART.

Strumble Head

Pembrokeshire

Headland, 5 miles (8km) northwest of Fishguard

This is the wild side of the Pembrokeshire coast. The headland cliffs tower above the pounding Atlantic surf, the path cuts an airy, at times precarious line, across their tops and the sky is alive with the sound of seabirds. Atlantic grey seals, porpoises and even dolphins are regularly spotted in the turbulent waters. Garn Fawr, a formidable rocky tor that lords high above the whole peninsula, brings a touch of hill walking to the experience, and the shapely lighthouse flashes a constant reminder of just how dangerous these spectacular waters can be.

Built in 1908 to help protect the ferries that run between Fishguard and Ireland, Strumble Head Lighthouse guards a hazardous stretch of coast that wrecked at least 60 ships in the 19th century alone. The revolving lights, which flash four times every 15 seconds, were originally controlled by a massive clockwork system that needed rewinding every 12 hours. This was replaced in 1965 by an electrically powered system and the lighthouse was then converted to unstaffed operation in 1980.

This is one of the best places along the Pembrokeshire coast to spot Atlantic grey seals. These lumbering marine giants can reach over 8ft (2.5m) in length and can weigh as much as 770lb (350kg). They are usually seen bobbing up and down (bottling) in the water just off the coast, but in the autumn, when the females give birth to a single pup, they often haul up on to inaccessible beaches, where the young are suckled on milk with an incredibly high fat content. The pups shed their white coat after around three weeks, when they are weaned and taught to swim before being abandoned. The males are usually bigger than the females, with a darker coat and a much more pronounced 'Roman' nose.

STRUMBLE HEAD LIGHTHOUSE GUARDS A ROCKY HEADLAND NEAR GOODWICK.

THE LIGHTHOUSE IS VISIBLE FROM THE PEMBROKESHIRE COASTAL PATH.

St David's

Pembrokeshire

15 miles (24km) southwest of Fishguard

In the 19th century, when Sir George Gilbert Scott was restoring St David's Cathedral, human bones were found hidden in a recess behind the high altar. They were the remains of two people, and perhaps three, and the probability is that these were the bones of St David himself and two other local saints, secreted away during the Reformation. Certainly the existence today of Britain's smallest city – really no more than a village – bears witness to the lasting influence of Wales's favourite saint, who founded a monastery here in the 6th century, and whose feast day on 1 March has become a rallying day for Welsh patriotic feeling. Celtic Christianity communicated by sea and this remote part of the Welsh coast was then a hub of missionary travel between Ireland, Wales, the southwest of England and Brittany.

David (Dewi in Welsh) is the only Welsh saint to have been canonised by the Roman Catholic Church, and in 1120 Pope Calixtus II ruled that two pilgrimages to distant St David's should count as equal to one pilgrimage to Rome. Pilgrims did indeed flock to the spot and it was their offerings that paid for the cathedral, Wales's largest church, which is tucked away in a dip by the little River Alun. It dates from all periods since the 12th century, and a striking

FAR RIGHT: THE VIEW FROM THE COASTAL PATH AT WHITESAND BAY, ST DAVID'S.

RIGHT: THE CITY'S COASTLINE IS PART OF PEMBROKESHIRE NATIONAL PARK.

feature of the Norman nave is its pronounced slope, with a rise of 14ft (4m) from the west end to the high altar. The impressive bishop's throne of about 1500 stands almost 30ft (10m) tall, and in front of the high altar is the tomb

of Edmund Tudor, father of Henry VII. Across the stream is the ruined Bishop's Palace. Bishop Barlow in the 16th century found himself with five daughters who needed dowries, so he gradually stripped the lead off the roof and sold it. (Suitably provided for, they all five went on to marry bishops.)

Other pleasures of a visit to this historic and tranquil place include not one but two aquariums (the Marine Life Centre and the Oceanarium), the rare breed animals at the Farm Park and the bygones in the Lleithyr Farm Museum. There are boat trips to Ramsey Island from the St Justinian lifeboat station and attractive walks along the cliffs. This area is part of the Pembrokeshire Coast National Park, which was set aside to protect some of the most impressive and beautiful coastal scenery in Britain. With a wealth of birdlife and plants, there are also remains of centuries of human activity, including kilns, quays and warehouses.

Pembrokeshire Coast National Park
Pembrokeshire

THE COASTAL PATH
AFFORDS VIEWS OF
RUGGED MILL BAY
AT ST ANNS HEAD.

THE BEAUTIFUL SANDY COVE AT MANORBIER IS POPULAR WITH FAMILIES AND SURFERS ALIKE.

The Pembrokeshire Coast National Park – at 225 square miles (583 sq km) one of the smallest of Britain's national parks – is the only one that is largely on the coast. Its main glory is its superb 230-mile (370km) coastline, which is followed for most of its way by the Pembrokeshire Coast Path, a wonderful rollercoaster of a walk with rugged cliffs, secluded sandy bays and the ever-changing seascapes.

The 170 miles (274km) of the Pembrokeshire Coast Path, which runs from St Dogmael's to Amroth, also offers a crash course in geology, for the route shows at a glance the story of the formation of the earth, from the earliest pre-Cambrian rocks around the tiny cathedral city of St David's to the Ordovician volcanic structure that underpins the northern area. The other great joy of walking the Coast Path National Trail is the variety of birdlife. The steep cliffs and sea stacks, such as those found around Govan's Head and Castlemartin, are the home to the rare, red-beaked chough, the most acrobatic of the crow family, as well as the kittiwake, guillemot and razorbill, the plump, penguin-like emblem of the National Park.

The only real uplands in this mainly coastal park are at the Preseli Hills in the north, a self-contained moorland block of Ordovician rocks rising to 1,759ft (536m) at Foel Cwm Cerwym, south of Bryberian. The Preseli Hills are famous as the source of the bluestones transported to Wiltshire for the inner circle of Stonehenge.

THE COASTAL PATH RUNS NEAR NEWGALE; NEWGALE SANDS IS AN ATTRACTIVE BEACH WORTH DETOURING FROM THE PATH FOR.

MARLOES SANDS IS KNOWN FOR ITS SANDY BEACH AND ITS CLIFFS WITH UNUSUAL ROCK FORMATIONS.

Skomer and Skokholm

Pembrokeshire

Islands off southwest coast of Wales at south end of St Bride's Bay

SKOMER ISLAND-
BOUND: PASSENGERS AT
MARTIN'S HAVEN
EMBARK FOR A TRIP.

These two island reserves off the western tip of the Pembrokeshire mainland are (together with the more remote Grassholm Island, an RSPB reserve and the site of the largest gannetry in England and Wales) one of Europe's foremost breeding sites for sea birds. Porpoises and dolphins are also regular visitors.

Skokholm has the first bird observatory built in Britain, founded here in the 17th century. Comical puffins and the rare Manx shearwaters nest in burrows on the island, together with colonies of guillemots, razorbills and storm petrels and about 160 grey seal pups, born each year off Skomer, a National Nature Reserve.

SKOMER ISLAND-BOUND: PASSENGERS AT MARTIN'S HAVEN EMBARK FOR A TRIP.

Milford Haven

Pembrokeshire

9 miles (15km) west of Pembroke

The Western Cleddau, the Eastern Cleddau and several lesser streams combine to form the huge natural harbour of Milford Haven. Viking fleets wintered here and medieval English expeditions mustered here to invade Ireland. The Dale and Angle peninsulas (both names are Norse) guard the entrance, reinforced in the 19th century by a bristling array of forts. The Dale Peninsula is both the sunniest place in Wales and the windiest, but the sheltered waters in the haven have made Dale itself a busy sailing and watersports centre. Nearby is the spot in Mill Bay where Henry Tudor landed in 1485 on his way to win the throne of England.

Milford Haven was laid out as a planned dockyard town 200 years ago, and the first inhabitants, astonishingly, were Quaker whaling families who immigrated here from Nantucket. Their meeting house dates from 1811. The story of the town is told in the Heritage and Maritime Museum, and the Haven Lightship is open to visitors. In the 1960s Milford Haven developed as a port for giant oil tankers.

FAR LEFT: INDUSTRIAL CHIMNEYS PROVIDE AN UNLIKELY FUTURISTIC BACKDROP TO THE HARBOUR.

LEFT: MODERN MARINA DEVELOPMENT HAS ENHANCED THE BEAUTY OF THIS HISTORIC FISHING VILLAGE.

Tenby

Pembrokeshire

9 miles (14km) east of Pembroke

SMALL BOATS NESTLE IN TENBY'S SHELTERED HARBOUR BELOW CASTLE HILL. WITH ITS THREE SANDY BEACHES, TENBY IS ONE OF THE UK'S MOST DELIGHTFUL RESORTS.

People have been singing Tenby's praises enthusiastically since the 9th century, when an anonymous Welsh poet composed verses in honour of the fine fortress on the bright headland and the courage and generosity of its late lord, a chieftain named Bleiddudd. More recent eulogies focus on the beauty of the old harbour lying in the headland's shelter, the handsome Regency houses overlooking it and the charm of medieval Tenby, with its narrow streets hemmed in by town walls that are the best preserved in South Wales. The famous Five Arches form the barbican to the old south gate. The walls were built in the 13th century and later strengthened, but were still not adequate to withstand Parliamentary artillery in the siege of 1644, when the town quickly surrendered.

Tenby was a prosperous fishing and cargo port, and at one time a smuggling haven for brandy brought across from France. The castle ruins on the headland today are not those of Bleiddudd's fortress, but of the later, medieval castle, built after Norman barons had conquered this part of Wales. The museum, housed in part of the castle remains, covers the local history, and there is a good collection of pictures by Welsh artists, including Augustus John (born in Tenby in 1878) and his sister Gwen, who grew up here. Also born in Tenby, in 1510, was Robert Recorde, the mathematician who invented the sign = for 'equals'. There is a memorial to him in St Mary's, claimed to be the largest parish church in Wales and a mark of Tenby's medieval prosperity. Another is the Tudor Merchant's House, the home of a well-to-do

businessman of about 1500, and probably the oldest house in the town.

Early in the 19th century Sir William Paxton, a wealthy banker, began to convert Tenby into a charming seaside resort which attracted many Victorian visitors. He built Laston House for the indoor seawater swimming baths, with a Greek inscription on the building meaning, 'The sea washes away all mankind's ills.' Today, besides sandy beaches for washing away the ills, Tenby offers visitors water sports, golf, fishing and an aquarium. There are boat trips to Caldey Island, where the monks at the Cistercian monastery (open to male visitors only) make perfumes from the wildflowers.

A HOST OF GOLDEN DAFFODILS

Tenby used to be known for its own special brand of wild daffodils, whose trumpets pointed upwards. They flowered early and were admired for their particularly vibrant colour. Demand for them was so strong that in the 1880s and 1890s half a million bulbs were sent up to London every year, and the plant came close to extinction.

IN PRAISE OF TENBY

'You may travel the world over, but you will find nothing more beautiful: it is so restful, so colourful and so unspoilt.'

Augustus John

Gower Peninsula

Swansea

Scenic area west of Swansea

WORMS HEAD
STRETCHES OUT
INTO THE SEA
NEAR RHOSSILI.

RHOSSILI BAY IS
THE MOST WESTERLY
BAY ON THE
GOWER PENINSULA.

The stubby Gower Peninsula, jutting 14 miles (23km) into Carmarthen Bay from Swansea, was in 1956 designated to be the first official Area of Outstanding National Beauty. The peninsula's unspoilt coastline has two distinct sides to its personality. In the south and southwest towering limestone cliffs are broken by a succession of sheltered sandy bays. North Gower, in contrast, has a low-lying coastline fringed with saltings and marshland.

The most spectacular part of the peninsula lies in the far west around Rhossili, where the land ends in the narrow promontory of Worm's Head. To the north are the dunes of Whiteford Burrows, the transition zone between spectacular and sedate Gower.

Most visitors head for south Gower. The main beaches here can become busy on summer weekends, although those prepared to walk — no hardship, for the coast paths along the cliffs are a joy in themselves — will find a quieter spot. Unexplored north Gower should not be ignored. These are atmospheric views across the peaceful saltings from ruined Weobley Castle, while further east the sands at Penclawdd are still scoured by the village's hardy cockle-pickers.

Swansea

Swansea

35 miles (56km) west of Cardiff

SWANSEA'S DOCKLAND AREA HAS BEEN REDEVELOPED AS AN ATTRACTIVE MARINA.

It was said that the only good thing from Swansea was the road out, but the poet Dylan Thomas's 'ugly, lovely town' – he was born here in 1914, at 5 Cwmdonkin Drive, and played in Cwmdonkin Park – has begun to recover in style from its painful post-war collapse as a premier industrial port. The new Maritime Quarter, created in the 1980s, has brought the old South Dock, off the River Tawe (the city's Welsh name is Abertawe), back to life as a marina. The quarter is equipped with lively new architecture that is positively pleasurable to look at, a big leisure centre, a theatre and pleasant places to eat and drink. The Maritime and Industrial Museum has a working woollen mill inside,

historic vessels to explore on the dock alongside, and lots of industrial machinery and transport exhibits. A short way inland is the splendid covered market, in a modern building but wholeheartedly traditional in spirit, and purveying Welsh lamb, seaweed laver bread and local cockles in ample quantities. Dignified Swansea Museum was the first in Wales, and the Glynn Vivian Art Gallery has delightful Swansea and Nantgarw porcelain to add to its pictures and sculptures. Many prehistoric remains from the caves and burial grounds of Gower are to be found in the Royal Institute of South Wales. There are sandy beaches along the shore and all the scenic beauty of the Gower Peninsula is in easy reach.

Cardiff

Cardiff

21 miles (34km) southeast of Merthyr Tydfil

In fewer than 200 years Cardiff has changed radically – twice. It was an inconspicuous port with a population of 1,000 in 1801 when the Industrial Revolution transformed it into one of the world's greatest coal ports, as the pits in the valleys to the north poured 'black diamonds' into it like water into a funnel. Then oil replaced coal, and since the 1950s Cardiff has turned itself into an engaging capital city for Wales.

Products of the 20th century include the noble Civic Centre, the National Museum of Wales and the delightful Welsh Folk Museum at St Fagans. The Welsh National Opera has its headquarters in Cardiff, and St David's Hall is a temple of music, as Cardiff Arms Park was of rugby. Excellent shopping, Victorian arcades and beautiful parks help to make this one of Britain's most enjoyable cities.

ABOVE: THE MILLENNIUM STADIUM, BUILT FOR THE RUGBY WORLD CUP IN 1999 IS A MAJOR FEATURE OF THE CARDIFF SKYLINE.

LEFT: THE PIERHEAD BUILDING FACING THE CARDIFF DOCKS WAS OPENED IN 1897.

Index